Insight VCE Revision Questions

English Language Units 3 & 4

First published in 2024
Insight Publications Pty Ltd
3/350 Charman Road
Cheltenham Victoria 3192
Australia

Tel: +61 3 8571 4950
Email: books@insightpublications.com.au

www.insightpublications.com.au

Insight VCE Revision Questions: English Language Units 3 & 4

ISBN: 9781923154940

Written and reviewed by Prudence Meggitt and Siegrid Fischer
Edited by Anica Boulanger-Mashberg
Proofread by Julia Carlomagno
Cover design and internal layout by Melisa Paredes
Internal design by Bec Yule @ Red Chilli Design
Printed by Markono Print Media Pte Ltd

Insight Publications acknowledges the Traditional Custodians of the Country on which we meet and work, the Boonwurrung People of the Kulin Nation. We pay our respects to their Elders past and present, and extend that respect to all Aboriginal and Torres Strait Islander Peoples.

Aboriginal and Torres Strait Islander readers should be aware that this publication contains names of deceased persons.

Contents

Introduction

Insight's *VCE Revision Questions: English Language Units 3 & 4* contains questions, suggested responses and tips to develop skills for assessment. We recommend using this resource as part of your study regime by completing sets of questions, as this process of applying your understanding and actively recalling information assists with deeper learning. You will also be able to review your answers and assess their appropriateness and accuracy against the provided responses. Note that this resource complies with the 2024–2028 VCE English Language Study Design.

The study of VCE English Language enables you to consider your understanding and application of English using a set of metalinguistic tools informed by the discipline of linguistics. This focus provides you with fresh insights into your language choices, the values and assumptions constructed when considering the language use of others, and the power of language to control, shape and disrupt our lives. In this resource, you will engage with the ways in which language is structured, the variations of language created by social and cultural difference, the nexus between language and power, and the ways in which language can be used to construct and deconstruct identity.

By using *VCE Revision Questions: English Language Units 3 & 4* as part of your study regime throughout the year, you will be prepared for questions you may encounter in your end-of-year VCE examination.

We wish you well with your studies.

The Insight Team

Questions

Section A: Short answer

Instructions

- Questions in Section A relate to Texts A–G.
- In your responses, you are expected to:
  - » demonstrate your ability to use relevant, descriptive and appropriate metalanguage
  - » demonstrate familiarity with the topics of Unit 3, 'Language variation and purpose', and the topics of Unit 4, 'Language variation and identity'.
- The set of questions for each text is worth 15 marks.

TEXT A

The following transcript is of an acceptance speech given at the 2015 Australian of the Year Awards. It is spoken by the Senior Australian of the Year, author and national Children's Laureate, Jackie French.

The following symbols are used in the transcript:

/	rising pitch
\	falling pitch
=	elongated sound
.	final intonation
(.)	short pause
(..)	medium pause
(…)	long pause
(H)	audible inhalation
<u>word</u>	emphatic stress
<A word A>	fast pace in relation to surrounding talk
<L word L>	slow pace in relation to surrounding talk
{*word*}	paralinguistic features

1. When (.) I was sixteen\ (..)
2. I thought (.) we could change the world\
3. when I was thirty-one/ (H)
4. I doubted\
5. but now I'm sixty-one/ (H)
6. I know\ we have done it\. (.)
7. Forget <A failure is not an option A> (H)
8. failure\ (.) is option one to a hundred/
9. but when you get to that hundred and first/(..) {*gestures with index finger*}
10. it (.) is (.) worth it. (..)
11. Yes/ (.) a book can change a child's life/ (..)
12. a book\ (.) can change the world/ {*smiles*}
13. (H) Every book a chi=ld reads\ <L creates new neurons L> in that child's brain\
14. If you want intelligent children\ (.)
15. give them a book\ (..)
16. If you want more intelligent children/ (H)
17. give them more books/
18. There is no such thing as reading difficulties\(.)
19. <L There are only teaching challenges L>.
20. (H) But humans are good at challenges\
21. We are descended from thos=e who survived the ice age\ (..)
22. (H) We are descended either from heroes\ (H)
23. or people who are very good at running very (.) very (.) fast. (...) {*smiles*}
24. {audience applause}
25. And a=s I reach (.)
26. what I would prefer= to call the <A afternoon tea A> of life\ (H)
27. I know= that this= (.) is what (.) we afternoon tea-ers
28. <L need to teach L> (..) our children\
29. That yes/(.) the most fulfilling <A thing of all A>
30. (H) is to hold our hands out to each other in friendship/(..)
31. not in hatred (.) not in division/(.)
32. To hold our hands out (.) {*holds hand out*} and say yes\
33. That hundred and first ti=me\
34. <L we will change L> the world (..) and it will be extraordinary.

Source: <https://www.youtube.com/watch?v=Kuc4GUfE3IM>

Question 1 (2 marks)

Discuss **one** way that information flow contributes to cohesion in lines 1–5. Use appropriate metalanguage and evidence of a specific discourse strategy to support your answer.

Question 2 (4 marks)

Explain how semantic patterning supports the speaker's purpose in lines 22–28. Use appropriate metalanguage in your response.

Question 3 (4 marks)

Discuss the use of modal verbs and verb tense in the text. Use appropriate metalanguage in your response.

Question 4 (5 marks)

With reference to prosodic and/or paralinguistic features and using appropriate metalanguage, explain a function of the text.

TEXT B

The following text is a campaign letter sent to residents of Eltham, Montmorency, Greensborough, Research, St Helena, Lower Plenty, Briar Hill, Greenhills and Eltham North in the lead-up to the 2018 Victorian state election. The original letter contains two artist-drawn eucalyptus tree branches in the top-right and bottom-left corners, respectively. The bottom-right corner of the letter has a picture of a smiling Nick McGowan, the Liberal Party candidate for the area, in a green t-shirt.

Save

Eltham, Montmorency Greensborough

Research, St Helena, Lower Plenty, Briar Hill, Greenhills and Eltham North

Traffic congestion is worsening locally. It's reducing our quality of life. It must be addressed, and requires a serious plan that includes road and importantly – rail.

Daniel Andrews says he will NOT duplicate our rail to Eltham Station if re-elected. This means Eltham and Monty station commuters will be forced to wait almost twice as long for trains as peak-hour commuters in Greensborough, and will never get a reliable 10-minute service.

At the same time, Labor also plans to reduce the number of car parks at Greensborough station* making it even harder to catch the train from there.

Monty Station also gets short-changed under Labor – no new car parks, no new station.

A vote for me in November is a vote for CRITICAL rail duplication to Eltham station while keeping and protecting the trestle bridge and IMPORTANTLY building 150 new free car parks across Greensborough, Montmorency and Eltham stations.

I am 100% committed to tackling local traffic congestion by road and RAIL.

Nick McGowan

Liberal for Eltham

*Andrews Government North-East Link business case as reported in the Diamond Valley Leader, June 20 2018.

Source: Nick McGowan, Liberal Party of Victoria

Question 1 (2 marks)

Analyse **one** syntactic pattern used in the discourse, using appropriate metalanguage.

Question 2 (2 marks)

Identify **one** informal language feature and comment on how it contributes to a purpose or intent of the discourse. Use appropriate metalanguage in your response.

Question 3 (4 marks)

Using appropriate metalanguage, identify and comment on the uses of passive voice in lines 6–11.

Question 4 (3 marks)

Using appropriate metalanguage, comment on **two** language features that reflect Nick McGowan's identity.

Question 5 (4 marks)

Using appropriate metalanguage, analyse how formatting and inference contribute to coherence in the text.

TEXT C

The following transcript is from an interview with Dylan Alcott (DA) by Channel 9 *Today Show* journalist and news presenter Tom Steinfort (TS). They are in London discussing Alcott's ninth Grand Slam wheelchair tennis win at Wimbledon.

The following symbols are used in the transcript:

<A A>	allegro – fast-paced utterance	(.)	very short pause
/	rising pitch	(..)	short pause
\	falling pitch	=	elongation of sound
.	final intonation	(H)	intake of breath
,	continuing intonation	@@@	laughter
?	questioning intonation	[ ]	overlapping of utterance
___	emphasis		

TS:	Dylan (.) congratulations
	Decent night of partying?
DA:	Ma=te (..) I'm feelin' a bit average
	[but I think that's deserved]
TS:	[@@@]
DA:	uh it's not every day you win the first ever (..)
	Wimbledon (.) singles for for my classification in wheelchair tennis
	Mate, um I got a bit emotional yesterday
	and I definitely let it all out last night
	And uh yeah I'm feelin' feelin' (.) a bit dusty/
	But very good\
	(Video clip of Dylan Alcott)
TS:	Yeah what is it,
	nine grand slam singles titles now?
DA:	Yeah nine grand slam singles titles\
	<A Actually it was quite funny, A>
	after I won Wimbledon my dad came up in tears and hugged me
	and goes eight gra= eight grand slams
	I can't believe it
	I said uh that's nine, champion
TS:	[@@@]
DA:	[He cut] one off\
	Wimbledon put out a tweet saying I won the Dylan Slam/
	cos I currently hold all four grand slams at once/
	but no one cares about that unless you win the grand slam
	which is a=ll in one calendar year (.) you know
	the last to to do that was Rod Laver
	someone that (.) is a big hero of mine so (H)
	one more to go,
	US Open six weeks away\
	so I'll be puttin' my head down and trainin' hard for that.
TS:	I saw Ash Barty congratulate you on Twitter uh
	Hugh Jackman (.) congratulating you/ just uh a bit of hobnobbing there/
DA:	I gotta say I was uh
	we were at a pub before
	<A I was with my partner Chantelle A>

I'm like oh Hugh Jackman [just hit me up]

TS: [@@@]

DA: that doesn't happen every day so\

Fi=ve six years ago when I used to play tennis

there would be 10 people there

<A and they were my family A>

now there's packed stadiums

it's it's changed so much and the the Austrayan public

you know for people like Hugh Jackman and Ash Barty

you know (.) big names

to actually really care and and watch it and say (.) you play really well/

cos they actually watched the match and things like that (.)

it (.) really means a lot\

(Clip of Dylan playing live)

I just wanna lea=ve the sport in a better spot for the next generation of

young athletes/

And (.) ah yeah it's it's all happening

An' it's because of the support of so many org=

you know awesome organisations like the Wide World of Sports who (.)

<A you know A> they actually broadcast my match first (.) live

this year at the Australian Open

The first time my finals ever played live

And then here here over in the BBC/

they played it live (.)

because they saw how many people watched it back home you know

people are startin' to believe in it\

TS: Why do you think people have embraced it so much\

DA: I think I've always knew that the product is good

like we are elite athletes who (.)

train our backsides off and put on a show every single time that we play/

and it's so great that people are startin' to see that

and that it's (.) I guess I get a great feeling

that I give a return on investment to ticket holders broadcasters (.)

sponsors alike (.)

There's that (..)

used to be that warm fuzzy feeling (.) with Paralympics/
Oh you know (.)
look at the inspirational Paralympians
yeah I get that we (.) are inspirational
but we're also elite athletes that put on a show
that people want to watch it now/
it it really does mean the world to me
because we train as much as Roger Federer does\
as much as Serena Williams does\
and uh for people to see that now
and to go man (.) that guy kicks (..)
you know (.)
he dominates
it really makes me feel good.
I love being Austrayan cos Austrayans really get around you
and it's ah (..) yeah
I'm I'm really honoured I guess
to win the first one.

Source: <https://www.youtube.com/watch?v=UMlzy5isQYw&feature=youtu.be>
Reproduced by permission of The Footage Company / Nine Network Australia

Question 1 (3 marks)

Identify and comment on the use of **two** different prosodic features used in lines 15–34.

Question 2 (3 marks)

Identify the tenor of the discourse and explain how this influences the register. Refer to examples and use appropriate metalanguage in your response.

Question 3 (4 marks)

Using appropriate metalanguage and referring to at least **two** subsystems of language, discuss how the semantic field changes throughout the text.

Question 4 (5 marks)

Using appropriate metalanguage, analyse the features of Australian English in the discourse.

TEXT D

The following text is a post by the Alphington Neighbourhood Social Group on a social media app. The group is not-for-profit and managed by local residents. Members of the group can use the comment tool to respond to posts. Alphington is a suburb 7 km from Melbourne's Central Business District.

Alphington Neighbourhood Social Group

Hi Everyone!

We're starting up a local networking group for people that live in Alphington and surrounding areas. The aim of the group is to create a happier and more connected community following a tough couple of years. Yay!

To join the group, you just need to fill in a short survey – link below – telling us a bit about you. And it's FREE!

Community events

We're planning a range of activities including trivia nights, picnics, casual sporting competitions, book swaps, group walks, puppy play dates and much, much more ...

We're also seeking locals with special talents so we can run community events. This might be DIY workshops for bike maintenance or simple household jobs. Maybe a learning to knit group. Or even a sports skills training afternoon so we can all learn to kick a footy or dribble a soccer ball around cones. Sound good?

If you have other ideas you'd like to run by us, just direct message us and we can chat online. We're very much open to ideas from our community members!

Christmas party

The first event we'd like to invite you to is the Christmas party in the Park. On Saturday 18 December come down to Alphington Park from midday. The group will set up near the barbecues but bring a picnic rug or camp chairs just in case! It's a BYO event – so you'll need to provide your own food and drinks.

This is a community initiative so no profit will be made by any individuals who offer their services. It's all about building a happier and more connected neighbourhood and supporting each other.

Please note doggos and puppers are very welcome; however, they must be kept under control.

We look forward to catching up with you and wish you a safe and happy summer.

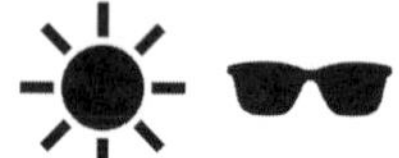

Alphington Neighbourhood Social Team

4 comments

John N. (Alphington)

Thanks for organising this!! Looking forward to Saturday and meeting new neighbours.

Anna Chew (Fairfield)

Great initiative 😊

Dhruv Rakesh (Alphington)

Will definitely attend with our dog, Edie! She looooooves to meet new people.

Mo A. (Alphington)

SAVE THE DATE! Twilight fete at the local children's centre in Feb 2022!

Question 1 (2 marks)

Analyse how **one** language feature reflects the register of the text.

Question 2 (3 marks)

Using appropriate metalanguage, describe the situational context of the text and explain the impact on **one** feature of coherence.

Question 3 (3 marks)

Using appropriate metalanguage, comment on the influence of technology on the language used.

Question 4 (3 marks)

Using appropriate metalanguage, compare the functions of the comments in lines 33–42.

Question 5 (4 marks)

Discuss how cohesion is achieved in the text. Use appropriate metalanguage, provide examples and refer to line numbers in your response.

TEXT E

The following text is a conversation between three work colleagues who are also friends. The conversation is taking place in a staffroom and the speakers involved are Ahana (A), Melinda (M) and Lin (L). They also refer to other work colleagues, Pari and Erika. Lin's partner, James, and Ahana's partner, Ross, are mentioned, too.

The following symbols are used in the transcript:

Symbol	Meaning	Symbol	Meaning
.	final intonation	(.)	very short pause
,	continuing intonation	(..)	long pause
?	questioning intonation	<A A>	allegro – fast-paced utterance
/	rising pitch	=	elongation of sound
\	falling pitch	@@@	laughter
___	emphasis	[ ]	overlapping utterance

L	I got one of these bottles/
	is that a (.) one of those insulated bottles?
M	Yep
L	Yep I got one\
	I got twenty dollars off/
A	How?
L	<A I found a voucher/ A>
	so it's getting sent to me,
	<A I was gonna get it sent here A>
	but it might not come on time\
	it says it'll come on Monday,
	but like I'm not trusting it just in case\
	but it's [got]
A	[No=] it should do,
	they're pretty [good]
L	[It's got] a gold bottom
	and a pink [top]
M	[Oooooo/]
A	[Yeah] I saw that
L	and I said to [Pari like]
A	[It's one] of the chrome ones\
	yeah?

L I was like I said to Pari <A is gold tacky? A>
cos you can't tell when you look online at the [picture]
M [No=]
A [No] it's not tacky
L and she was like no=
A Who's got the gold one?
I think Erika might have the gold [one\]
L [Okay]
A [I think]
L I am never telling James how much I spent on a bottle (..)
like I got it for (..)
what thirty-nine dollars instead of (.) whatever.
<A How much was yours? A>
M I think it was about that\
L @@ that's a bit rude of me to ask\
M @@@ nah nah
L Imagine\
he'd be like,
it's a water bottle (.) why did you spend forty,
almost forty dollars [on]
A [So] I didn't tell Ross how much I spent on
mine/
and then we went to like a homewares shop/
and they sold them [there/]
L [@@@]
A [and he's like]
that's your water bottle\
and I was like yeah it is <A but let's go and look at this/ A>
and he's like (.) I really hope they've got an insane price
mark up,
rather than the one [beside it\]
L [@@@]
A And I went mmm hmm hmm [sure]
L [sure]
A Yeah sure if that helps you sleep at night go for it.
L mmm so I was saying to Pari like is it worth it?

	and she's like yeah they're really [good]
M	[mmm]
L	they insulate like it's the best tasting water I've ever had\
A	Yeah it keeps it cold (..) for ages
L	and everyone at the gym has them.
M	I dropped my coffee one\
	and the uh (.) circumference [dinted]
L	[oh]
M	and now it doesn't seal anymore\
L	Oh no=
M	Yep.
A	um I told you what one of my girlfriends said/
	she reckons that it's a massive marketing ploy (.)
	that they make the lids of them (.) rea=lly fragile/
	because he said (..)
	they're selling you a sustainable product,
	you're going to be a one-time customer,
	and never come back and buy [again\]
M	[mmm/]
A	So if they make it that it's breakable,
	you have to then keep coming back buying it again and again and
	[again]
M	[yes]
A	and I was like oh my go=d,
	I've bought two lids for mine already [@@@]
M	[@@@]
L	[@@@]
	Maybe that's a business we need to get into\
	<A then we can retire\ A>
A	That's how you make money,
	come up with like a niche product
	or a niche [app].
M	[mmm]
L	James has a friend in England who makes apps,
	but he did say he feels like he just (.)
	he doesn't have a worthy (.) job/

95. he says I just go to work and (.) make lots of money,
96. and I don't really contribute to society\
97. and I'm like <A no you don't A>
98. A No=
99. It would be so [boring]
100. M [Mmmm]
101. L Like they've got a nice big house in Cheshire,
102. but but you know whatever.

Question 1 (2 marks)

Using appropriate metalanguage, identify and discuss the function of a prosodic feature between lines 43 and 54.

Question 2 (2 marks)

Analyse an example of turn-taking in relation to topic management in this conversation. Refer to line numbers and use appropriate metalanguage in your response.

Question 3 (3 marks)

How does the register of the discourse support a purpose or intent of the conversation? Refer to one discourse or language feature and use appropriate metalanguage in your response.

Question 4 (3 marks)

How does Lin negotiate her listeners' face needs between lines 31 and 41? Use appropriate metalanguage in your response.

Question 5 (5 marks)

Analyse the tenor and group identity of Lin, Melinda and Ahana in this conversation. Use appropriate metalanguage in your response.

TEXT F

Hector Light is a popular singer. Prior to the Melbourne leg of his Tour of Light concert in 2023, Ticketmaster sent ticketholders the following email containing information about the upcoming show. Light's album releases include *Hector's House* and his song titles include 'The Path' and 'Priceless'. He also has a line of fragrances and skin products called 'Delightful'.

ticketmaster

Hi Shareena,

Congrats! With patience, and maybe some tears you've managed to get your hands on the most sought after tour tickets in Australia!

After months of fantasising, Australian Hector fans are finally getting their turn to join the Tour of Light hype.

With Hector's arrival fast approaching we wanted to fill you in on the quickest way to get you into Hector's House and ready for the show.

All tickets are DIGITAL!

Firstly, all tickets purchased through Ticketmaster are digital*. This means you can easily access your tickets via the Ticketmaster app or mobile web browser via Ticketmaster.com.au, for the smoothest entry and to ensure you get in on time to see Hector add your tickets straight to your **phone's ticket wallet** and share them with your friends and family.

**excluding collector tickets*

Screenshotting is out

It's time to move into our solo artist era and stop screenshotting our tickets. Why? Because your time is Priceless, and nobody wants to be stuck at the entry gate behind the person with slow data problems or even worse, stuck behind someone scrolling endlessly through their photos to find a screenshot of their ticket.

Be smarter than that and use the app instead because it allows you to easily forward tickets to your friends and family or anyone joining you at the show.

It'll be – Delightful – for the environment if you don't print your tickets.

With Tour of Light partnering with organisations throughout the tour to make a positive environmental impact, we know Hector would be proud of you for using a digital ticket instead of wasting paper by printing your tickets.

Luckily you can forward your tickets to your friends via the app, and you no longer need to print them. Mobile tickets are a great environmentally friendly ticketing option.

But what if I've spent too long watching Hector thirst traps and my phone is out of battery? How do I access my ticket(s)?

If you are concerned about your phone battery on the day of the event, we suggest waiting to see Hector in person on stage instead of watching Tik Toks.

Alternatively, if your battery does run out of charge on the day, do not worry. The Ticketmaster support team located outside Gate 7 will be able to print you a replacement ticket for the day.

Still a bit sceptical?

Don't walk The Path of scepticism, when it comes to mobile tickets. There is nothing to be worried about because here's what other fans have had to say about mobile tickets.

> "Love mobile tickets! I have been using this for ages! Easy to share with friends. Save paper and ink. Don't have to worry about forgetting my tickets!"

> "Super convenient. I didn't have to be the responsible one for making sure everyone got their tickets all printed out. The mobile tickets mean that everyone had their tickets delivered safely."

If you want more information on mobile tickets, you can find it here.

Anything else you need to know?

As one of the world's most dedicated fandoms, we understand your enthusiasm to get to the show early to get the best spot possible. However, we want you to be safe and do not encourage camping out at the venue in the lead-up to the show. Each venue will have specific rules about camping. We encourage you to head to the website relevant to the venue you are attending for more information on what is allowed.

Our FAQ Page lists most of the common questions and latest event info. Add it to your bookmarks and stay on top of the latest news regarding your event. That's it for now, but if anything else comes up, we'll be in touch.

Enjoy the show,

Ticketmaster Fan Support Team

Source: Adapted from Ticketmaster

Question 1 (3 marks)

Identify **one** function of the text between lines 2 and 27 and comment on how this function is addressed. Use appropriate metalanguage in your response.

Question 2 (4 marks)

Analyse how Ticketmaster attempts to reduce the social distance and build rapport between themselves and the audience. Use appropriate metalanguage in your response.

Question 3 (3 marks)

Discuss the use of syntax between lines 16 and 23. Use appropriate metalanguage in your response.

Question 4 (5 marks)

Discuss the use of morphological and semantic patterning in the text. Use appropriate metalanguage in your response.

TEXT G

The Docklands is a suburb on the bay in Melbourne that sits on the edge of the city. It was the subject of a series of articles by *The Age* newspaper, exploring the area's history and how it might be improved in future. The following text is an editorial that is part of that series, published online.

We should dare to dream of a Docklands that isn't dreadful

By *The Age's* View

April 19, 2024 — 6.04pm

On the western edge of the city, at the mouth of Victoria Harbour, lies a perplexing planning and political legacy.

The Docklands may be only three decades young, but no other postcode in Melbourne draws views as varied and vitriolic as the waterside city suburb.

Many chalk Docklands up as a colossal policy failure that produced a windswept, avoidable eyesore. Others, especially many of the suburb's 16,000 residents, believe postcode 3008 is brimming with potential, needing only a smidgen of love to finally grow into the city jewel.

Whether the Docklands should be conceived as a concrete jungle or vibrant hub was the question driving a series published in The Age this week, with six stories examining some of the suburb's maligned hallmarks: Gale force winds, generic towers and the ominously motionless Melbourne Star observation wheel. It adds to a long history of *The Age's* deep reporting on the Docklands, including feature-length stories in 2006 and 2012.

As with most things, to understand what Docklands *is*, we must go back and consider how it first came to be. The Docklands' origin story begins with an ethereal vision to turn Melbourne's rust bucket image into a city of dreams.

It was 1989. The then-Labor Cain government wanted to transform the 200 hectares of toxic swamps and industrial wasteland into an inner-city oasis.

The planning blueprint at the time envisioned a sparkling waterfront with varied and rich architecture and buildings as modest as two to six storeys so as not to dominate the harbour.

The urban makeover would catapult Melbourne's reputation, rendering it a destination "many cities can only dream about", the blueprint stated.

But reality bit in the early 1990s when a deep recession gripped the state and the future of the Docklands fell into the hands of then-Liberal premier Jeff Kennett, who stamped the site with his signature free-market thinking. That turned Docklands into more of an experiment in laissez-faire urban development.

Unlike Cain's state-sponsored renewal of the development of Southbank along the Yarra River, Kennett withheld public subsidies from the Docklands, leaving the high-risk job of building on contaminated swampland to developers willing to cop the risk.

The land was released to the market all at once in what was described as an "instant city" approach – a new brand of building shaped and built by market interests with no government investment.

The fast-pace parcelling up and selling of chunks of land created a property boom and brought some initial economic gains, including a boost to employment.

But shortcomings in government planning, including for amenities like parks, schools and cultural sites as well as insufficient control on building heights and design, allowed for the proliferation of often mediocre apartment towers and corporate offices along the water's edge that maximised developers' profits while overlooking resident liveability. Docklands became less vibrant village and more dispiriting downtown.

There have undoubtedly been successful efforts to rejuvenate the area since, including the building of an award-winning library and a primary school that have been welcomed by the growing local community. Significant businesses have also been attracted to the precinct along with thousands of workers, as the supply of land next to the CBD also helped keep a lid on Melbourne's comparatively attractive office rents.

But in all, Docklands is today largely defined by its flaws. Instead of a green walkway that lines New York's Hudson River, or the floating turquoise pool built into an old cargo container on Berlin's Spree River, the Docklands is characterised by its maze of asphalt, empty shopfronts and concrete dead-ends.

What we have today is almost the antithesis of that late-80s vision.

At *The Age,* we believe that it is time to take a good look at the precinct and the ways that it can be improved. While it may be tempting for the current government to think that this is not a problem of their making, they would be wiser to view it as an opportunity rather than an inconvenience.

The Docklands should be a productive extension of the central city, connecting seamlessly to urban renewal projects such as Fishermans Bend, making it a gateway between the city and its growing surrounds.

Source: *The Age*'s View, 'We should dare to dream of a Docklands that isn't dreadful', *The Age*, <https://www.theage.com.au/national/victoria/we-should-dare-to-dream-of-a-docklands-that-isn-t-dreadful-20240418-p5fl0e.html>, 19 April 2024

Question 1 (2 marks)

Explain the effect of **one** example of phonological patterning used between lines 1 and 12. Use appropriate metalanguage in your response.

Question 2 (4 marks)

Discuss **two** different examples of sense relations in the text. Use appropriate metalanguage in your response.

Question 3 (4 marks)

Using appropriate metalanguage, discuss how tenor influences the register of the text.

Question 4 (5 marks)

Referring to lines 13–26 **or** 56–67, discuss the syntactic features of the text and how these are used to achieve a purpose or intent of the text. Use appropriate metalanguage in your response.

Section B: Analytical commentary

Instructions

- Section B relates to Texts H–N.
- Section B requires an analytical commentary on a text.
- In your response, you are expected to:
  - » demonstrate your ability to use relevant descriptive and metalinguistic tools
  - » demonstrate familiarity with the topics of Unit 3, 'Language variation and purpose', and the topics of Unit 4, 'Language variation and identity'.
- Each analytical commentary is worth 30 marks.

Analytical commentary (30 marks)

Write an analytical commentary on the language features of the text.

In your response, you should comment on the:

- function(s), purpose(s) and intent(s) of the text
- situational and cultural context(s) influencing and affecting the text
- the influence of register, tenor and audience
- relevant characteristics and features of language in the text.

Refer to at least **two** subsystems of language in your analysis.

TEXT H

The following transcript is of a promotional video called 'Faces of Aboriginal Businesses in Victoria: Clothing The Gap', produced by Business Victoria. In the video, the co-founders of the fashion label Clothing The Gaps (known as 'Clothing The Gap' when the video was released), Laura Thompson and Sarah Sheridan, discuss the values of their company and share advice about small business enterprise. This transcript includes references to multimedia aspects of the video (such as images and music). Uplifting music plays throughout.

The following symbols are used in the transcript:

__	emphasis
(.)	very short pause
(..)	short pause
<A A>	allegro (fast paced utterance)
[ ]	overlapping speech
=	elongated sound
@	laughter
/	rising intonation
\	falling intonation
,	continuing intonation
.	final intonation
[*multimedia*]	multimedia information

LT: Community's changing
and fashion's changing
so if you can wear an item of fashion (.) that's actually making a social
impact
why wouldn't you choose those brands?
[*image of models wearing Clothing The Gap t-shirts and hats*]
I'm Laura Thompson, <A I'm a Gunditjmara woman A>/
SS: and my name's Sarah Sheridan\
LT: And we're from Clothing The Gap.
SS: [*image of clothingthegap.com.au webpage scrolls up*] We produce Aboriginal
designed merchandise
LT: We're a small [start up/]
SS: [yeah]
LT: but we're completely committed to the cause

We spent a lot of time thinking about what should we call this business
and we've gone through a lot of names/ (.) in order to try'n tell and
<A express to non-Aboriginal people A> that we want youda wear our
stuff
[*Image of a smiling model and a social media post with 122 Likes*]
and when we come up with Clothing The Gap, it resonated with people/
[*Image of a model in the merchandise and a social media post:*
Omg need ♥♥♥]
that that was one way they could engage.
SS: And as a non-Aboriginal person I think it's really exciting to be able
t'produce a piece of (.) of clothing and fashion that everybody can
celebrate.
LT: Our typical/ customer now\ is any Austrayan who wants to make a
decision that when they purchase something that they're actually
making a difference/
and contributing to closing the gap.
[*music becomes more uplifting*]
We've had lots of experience producing merchandise
we love seeing Aboriginal design out in the community
[*image of Aboriginal artwork on clothing with a community member*
giving a thumbs up gesture]
That makes us feel good, it promotes Reconciliation
and in some small way, all of us can be part of celebrating Aboriginal
culcha
We make the most of every day in the office and the most of every
opportunity
if anyone rings our doorbell downstairs/
SS: They're coming up for a cuppa, no two days're the same
There's so much to lea=rn!
LT: Yep
SS: @@
We're doing the HR
we're sorting out accounting
we're (.) making sure that we're planning for the future as well cos we
wanna be here for a really long time

LT: Our succession plan is that Clothing The Gap will be able to support
the work we do at Spark Health in delivering health promotion and
prevention programs to Aboriginal communities all over Victoria/
SS: We absolutely love social media so social media is something that we
spend a lot of time thinking about/
and doing as well\ cos it's a genuine tool and a (.) a resource for us (.) in
communicating and getting our messages out as well.
LT: My cultural heritage (.) impacts me every day at work/
and I'm lucky that through Clothing The Gap I'm able to (..) create pieces (.) of
art/
or clothes where people are able to express their identity 'n culcha
through their garments and fashion/
It comes quite natural for us to be able to support Aboriginal
businesses and business people/
Where possible, we're always looking to employ Aboriginal people to
support the work we do
SS: There's nothin' better than being able to cheer on other Aboriginal
businesses as well
It's just awesome to see everyone kicking massive goals in this space
LT: You don't have to have all the answers at once
Once you start moving though the business you'll find the answers/
and that shouldn't be the reason why you don't move into that space.
SS: Yeah, and when it gets hard just focus on that end goal
know why you're in it
so for us it's the difference we're making in the community every day
that keeps us going.
LT: Clothing The Gap is one way that we can make sure that we're around
here to keep adding years to people's lives into the future/
[*Image of the words*:
Get behind
CLOTHINGTHEGAP
You can support us
www.clothingthegap.com.au]

Source: Business Victoria, <https://www.youtube.com/watch?v=LVXhqQQSvaU>, accessed 18 December 2023.

TEXT I

The following text is an article that featured on a Victorian high school's online bulletin in January 2023. It was posted a week before students were due to return to school for the 2023 academic year by Student Services.

Though the post is aimed at students, it was also available to be viewed by staff and the parent/carer community.

Tackling the Back-to-School Blues

Ah, summer – six weeks hanging out with family and friends. You might have even gotten a part-time job to build up some independence as well as your bank account (good for you!). Of course, the holidays can't last forever, and your mind has likely started fixating on that dreaded first day back at school. This can be doubly so if you're at – or about to start – HIGH SCHOOL. *Cue dramatic music*

Maybe you're thinking:

'I wish summer wasn't about to be over!' 'What if I don't make friends or the teachers aren't nice?' 'I've got to know what I want to do for VCE and I'm all out of ideas!'

These are all natural thoughts and will have crossed the minds of all your peers and friends at least once. Heck, some of your teachers will likely have thought, 'What if my students don't like me?'

Well, to ease the transition back to school life and develop good habits for the rest of the year, here are three suggestions that might help you:

Talk about your feelings

Created by Michele McDonald, a popular Buddhist teacher, the acronym RAIN (Recognise, Allow, Investigate, Nurture) is a simple way to mindfully explore your feelings, whether on your own or with a friend or adult you feel comfortable talking to. Labelling our emotions engages the thinking brain and works towards calming us down.

- RECOGNISE what you're feeling and name it. 'I feel scared' or 'I am nervous'.

- ALLOW your feelings to be there with you without judgement. Make room for them.
- INVESTIGATE gently and with curiosity why this feeling is there. 'Is it because I'm going into Year 9?'
- NURTURE yourself. What do you need to do to make yourself feel better – eat, sleep, exercise?

Make a timetable for outside of school

Yeah, your school timetable is probably waiting for you in your inbox. Still, a timetable doesn't have to be restricted to the classroom, and it can be helpful to stay organised at home. Think about when you want to get up in the morning and when you want to sleep. Then enter your other commitments, like footy training, volunteering, family time, etc. This will help you work out when you have time to complete your homework or revise. You might even schedule in the subjects you find more challenging in the morning to give yourself more time for those. Make sure to include relaxation time, too!

Maintain a regular sleep pattern

The holidays have meant staying up late, playing computer games, streaming on Twitch or binge-watching *Heartstopper*. So, the thought of going back to school and going to bed early is understandably not one we all relish. The thing is, research shows that adolescents and young adults need at least 7–9 hours of sleep a night. Therefore, a good sleeping routine will help you get the hours you need regularly. Let us start with the basics:

- Create a routine of setting your alarm for the same time every morning and going to bed at the same time every night. (Psst! This is where your timetable could help!)
- Lay off the sugar and caffeine before bed; they can make it harder to get to sleep.
- Keep calm, but yes, you should probably turn off your TV, mobile phone and laptop/tablet at least 30 minutes before bed because light from these devices can trick your brain into thinking it's still daytime, which can impact sleep. That said, you could create a sleep playlist with gentle music that will help slow your heart rate and help you unwind before bed.

We hope the above at least gets your brain tingling about what you could be doing to support yourself at school. Remember: 2020 to 2022 has been a rollercoaster for us all. As we enter 2023, be kind to yourself, try not to self-sabotage and celebrate those small victories in life. You just need to take it one day at a time. You got this!

The Student Services team

TEXT J

The following speech took place in the Senate in October 2021. Then-Leader of the Opposition in the Senate and Shadow Minister for Foreign Affairs, Penny Wong, was speaking to the senators during Youth Voice in Parliament Week. Part of Wong's speech uses the words of a young woman from Wong's electorate in South Australia, Winter Birkett.

The following symbols are used in the transcript:

<L L>	lento – slow-paced utterance	,	continuing intonation
<A A>	allegro – fast-paced utterance	.	final intonation
(.)	short pause	___	emphasis
/	rising pitch	-	truncated word
\	falling pitch	=	elongation of sound
(H)	intake of breath		

I am speaking today on behalf of uh (.)
A young Australian\
<A A young South Australian A>
As part of Youth Voice in Parliament Week.
Ms Winter Birkett is 17 years old,
and she lives in my duty electorate of Boothby, <A and these are her wo=rds A>.
As of August (.) Australia ranks 50th globally,
for the representation of women in national par=liaments\
<A It's 2021 A> and this statistic is (.) not (.) good enough\
(H)
It's not just that we can do better,
in terms of addressing the representation of women in Australian politics/

we must do better\
As such, in 20 yea=rs I want to live in an Australia where young girls,
of diverse backgrounds and from all all around the country,
aspire to one day become politicians.
(H)
I want to live in an Australia where instead of girls like me being actively
discouraged/
from pursuing politics because it is something for men,
and a (.) dirty ga=me\
girls are uplifted and empowered to do so.
I hope that in 20 yea=rs Australia will come to place,
significant value on young girls and women being politically ambitious/
However, to achieve this, the status quo must change\
Currently/ Australia's political culture <A sends a clear message to politically
interested girls A>
That politics is not for us\
And this message permeates through all levels of society,
stemming from parliament itself.
This narrative must be challenged (.) now,
so that in 20 years things change\
Because if not, Australia risks <L never achieving anything close L> to
gender equality\
(H)
Ms Birkett is ri=ght, we must do better.
The majority of senators are now women/
And that's because Labor now has more women than men in the Senate/
And that is because of our affirmative a-action targets\
So again/
I once again call on all Australia's political parties\
To mandate targets for <L equal women's representation L>.

Source: <https://www.youtube.com/watch?v=CQshG8zYdGQ>, 21 October 2021

TEXT K

The following press release appeared on the Parks Victoria website following a decision made in the Federal Court in relation to the protection of flora and fauna in the Alpine National Park, Victoria. A *brumby* is a feral horse found in Australia.

Protecting the Alpine National Park

Friday 8 May, 2020

Federal Court finds in favour of Parks Victoria

The Federal Court of Australia has today delivered its judgement in the case between Parks Victoria and the Australian Brumby Alliance (ABA), ruling in favour of Parks Victoria. Parks Victoria welcomes the decision from the Federal Court today which recognises the severe impacts of feral horses on the iconic Alpine National Park and allows horse control programs to resume.

The ABA had sought an injunction to stop Parks Victoria undertaking removal of feral horses from the Alpine National Park in accordance with its 'Protection of the Alpine National Park – Feral Horse Strategic Action Plan 2018–2021'. The question before the Court was whether the removal of horses by Parks Victoria challenged cultural heritage values associated with horses in the Alpine National Park, as defined under the *Environment Protection and Biodiversity Conservation Act 1999* (EPBC Act) and the National Heritage List.

Parks Victoria has an obligation to reduce the abundance of feral horses in Victoria's national parks as necessary to protect natural values and meet legislative obligations.

His Honour Justice O'Bryan stated, 'I am not satisfied that the Action, involving the removal of brumbies from the Bogong High Plains and the reduction in number of brumbies in the Eastern Alps, will have or is likely to have a significant impact on the National Heritage values of the Australian Alps.'

Over the past 18 months, the injunction led to Parks Victoria suspending the majority of the alpine feral horse management operation. Trapping and rehoming programs that were previously implemented were put on hold, subsequently limiting the effectiveness in significantly reducing the feral horse population and environmental damage to the fragile wildlife, plants and habitats in the Victorian Alps.

During this period, a comprehensive aerial survey across the Australian Alps found a significant increase in feral horse numbers, 2 to 3 times higher than in the previous survey (estimates rising from 9000 to 24 000 horses over five years). Additionally, the bushfires over the 2019–20 summer have greatly impacted large areas of the Victorian Alps, resulting in significant loss of threatened native wildlife and ecosystems. Remaining unburnt areas are being severely overgrazed and damaged by large numbers of feral horses.

Given the current circumstances, Parks Victoria will be commencing an additional technique to control horses. Small-team operations will be deployed into high-conservation priority locations where ground-based professional shooters will use thermal imaging and noise suppressors to cull free-ranging feral horses, under strict animal welfare protocols with expert equine veterinary oversight. This will complement the current bushfire recovery works that have removed more than 1300 deer from fire-impacted areas in eastern Victoria.

The longer-term program of trapping and rehoming of feral horses will continue. You can read about the rehoming process, and how to submit an expression of interest at www.parks.vic.gov.au/get-into-nature/conservation-and-science/conserving-our-parks/feral-animals

Media enquiries

Stephanie Zilles

TEXT L

The following text is an excerpt from the foreword to Nakkiah Lui's print version of her play, *Black is the New White*. It is a play about love, politics and family. Lui is a playwright, writer, commentator and actor. She is also a winner of the Nick Enright Prize for Playwriting, NSW Premier's Literary Awards. Lui is a Gamilaroi/Torres Strait Islander woman, and a leader in the Australian Aboriginal community.

I love Christmas. My family love Christmas. I have never missed a Christmas with my family. That would be akin to some kind of sacrilege. I love the excitement you get from putting up the tree, singing along to Christmas carols that you only know two lines of. I love wrapping presents and trying to curl the ribbon just right. I love shopping with my family in the overcrowded shopping centres with their too-cold air conditioning and getting a kebab from the food court. I love the smells of cooking all day and getting dressed up to not leave the house. I love watching Christmas movies from the northern hemisphere that are filled with snow and cosiness, whilst I sweat it out in front of a fan. I love being with my family. A family that is changing as we get older, new members and additions joining each year and sometimes, sadly, a loved one leaving.

But Christmas isn't where the play started. That's where the play ended up. *Black is the New White* started as two separate conversations. The first was about love. I was having a conversation with a cousin of mine who is this fabulous young Aboriginal woman, a gorgeous and great mum, a lover of Instagram and lycra and the hashtag #yummymummy. We were talking politics (talking politics is like talking sports in my family) and for some reason love came up, and she said that communities should try to stick together, to 'get bigger and better and Blacker' ... her racial/political beliefs could be seen as akin to Black separatism and I didn't necessarily agree with her (I had dated one Aboriginal person and not had much luck – they turned out to be a cousin).

However, at the same time, both my parents are Aboriginal, same as hers, so why did she hold those beliefs and why didn't I? I thought it was a really interesting conversation to be having with someone who, I would say, is part of this new emerging Aboriginal middle class. It was around this time that I looked at the census and discovered a surprising statistic: 74 per cent of Aboriginal people who get married marry non-Aboriginal people. We were the community most likely to marry a race outside of our own. I found this really interesting ... it intrigued me as to who this 74 per cent are.

Primarily because I was one of them. I fell in love as I started writing this play. I'd got engaged by the time it had finished. To a White man. I was part of this 74 per cent ... but that really bothered me, because, to me, my love was way more than a statistic. But there it was ... an overwhelming statistic that was vastly different to the trends of non-Aboriginal Australians.

That led me to investigate how my own family had shifted over the last two generations, and how this had affected their definition of class. I was really interested in how we identify ourselves in terms of our racial and cultural backgrounds, and how that intersects with class. What does it mean to be successful? Especially as Aboriginal people, when you come from a community that is so often politicised. I also wanted to present a family of Aboriginal people that hasn't been seen before, not just on stage, I would say, but within the canon of Australian artistic works. That is, an Aboriginal family who have money, who are not necessarily oppressed, but are culturally quite strong. So I had the idea of putting forth that family, because, for me, that was similar to what I've grown up with.

Source: Nakkiah Lui, *Black is the New White*, Allen & Unwin, Crows Nest (NSW), 4 February 2019

TEXT M

The following transcript is an extract from the television show *Q+A*, an Australian television panel discussion program broadcast on the ABC (Australian Broadcasting Corporation). This episode aired on 8 October 2018 and focused on good teaching. The chair was Tony Jones (TJ), an Australian journalist. This portion of the show features panellist Eddie Woo (EW), award-winning classroom and YouTube maths teacher. Miriam Lees (ML) is an audience member; audience members on *Q+A* participate by asking questions of the invited guests.

The following symbols are used in the transcript:

Symbol	Meaning	Symbol	Meaning
.	final intonation	__	emphatic stress
=	lengthening of a sound	[ ]	onset and duration of simultaneous speech
,	continuing intonation		
?	questioning intonation	@@	laughter
\	falling pitch	<A A>	allegro – fast-paced utterance
/	rising pitch	<H>	audible breath
--	truncated intonation	(( ))	vocal effects, non-verbal communication or transcriber comment
-	truncated word		
(.)	very short pause		
(..)	medium pause		

TJ: Good evening/ and welcome to this (.) special *Q+A* focused on good
teaching/
I'm Tony Jones\ here to answer your questions, teacher turned
champion of the Finnish education system (.) Pasi Sahlberg\
Centre for Independent Studies education research fellow (.)
Jennifer Buckingham\
primary school teacher Gabbie Stroud/
who quit the profession she loved in frustration\ (.)
award-winning classroom and YouTube maths teacher/ (.) Eddie Woo\
(.) and Indigenous teacher and advocate (.) Cindy Berwick\
please welcome our panel\
((audience applauds))
TJ: <A Thank you very much A>
Now, *Q+A* is live in eastern Australia on ABC TV (.) iview and
News Radio\
Well tonight with Year 12 final exams in sight
we have gathered a stellar panel and an audience full of eager
students/ parents/ (.) and teachers\ to talk about better schools\

and our first question/ (.) comes from Miriam Lees.
ML: Hey (.) go- good evening/
Um/ (.) it's not OK to say/
I can't read/
but it's OK to say/
I can't do maths\
Why do you think that's the case?
TJ: Eddie (.) we'll start with you, obviously/
EW: <H> (.) as a mathematics teacher
having heard this (..) statement <A many, many A> times,
I feel as thou=gh there's a s- sense of frustration boiling in my mind,
because I (.) struggled with mathematics when I was at school/
a=nd so [to be able to sa=y]
TJ: [so wait you weren't] a maths genius when you were at school?
EW: No= and I'm @@still @not a maths @genius now/
uh but for me that always/ felt a little bit like an excuse\
and then I realised (.) I think (.) Miriam
that in many ways there was a uh a sense of (.) wanting to have
a reason (..)
wanting to have a- uh- almost <H>
not an excuse but a reason to sa=y,
'look this is something that I've struggled with'
mathematics is hard\
mathematics is abstract\
it is-- you know
for the last 300 years,
all the mathematics that we've invented as human beings
have been things that regular people on the street have
found (.) mind-blowing\
and so we want a reason to be able to say,
'yeah that was too hard for me'
and I think the reason that we grab for is,
'it's just not my thing\'
'it was genetics\'
'it was society\'
and so I think it's almost as though
w- we're looking for something (.) to comfort us/

to say/
this is difficult (.)
there was a reason why (.)
and it didn't have to do with me\
TJ: Now Eddie
it wasn't my thing either as it turns out
even though my dad was a maths teacher\
but I do remember from school
<A the square on the hypotenuse
equals the sum of the squares on the other two sides/ A>
and I didn't really understand it until I saw your WooTube version
of this\
now, how is it that you can explain things that many other people
struggle with?
EW: Well (.) in fa- I think (.) struggle (.) actually (.) is the key\
because at school (.) the humanities
<A English, History and Drama A>
were the subjects that I enjoyed most Tony,
despite the fact that your dad wrote some of the textbooks.
<A Jones and Couchman, if anyone appreciates that classic A>
((audience laughs))
TJ: Modern Mathematics\
EW: <A It was a classy, classy work\ A>
but that struggle that I experienced as a student
I still carry with me now after more than 10 years of teaching
and so (.) I can actually look at a st- student
at- a- the look in their eyes
and I can say (.)
I know what that feels like\
and I think that empathy is the key ingredient (.) of great teaching\
TJ: You would have seen that look in my eyes @@many times
if I'd been in your @@maths classes\
((audience laughs))
TJ: not to worry about that\
Cindy Berwick, now you were a maths teacher for 20 years\

Source: *Q+A* Teaching Special, 8 October 2018, ABC. Reproduced by permission of the Australian Broadcasting Corporation – Library Sales. QandA © 2018 ABC

TEXT N

The following excerpt from a press release was published by the ABC on its website in 2017. The Hottest 100 is a series of songs chosen by listeners to the ABC's youth radio station, triple j, at the end of each year. In previous years, the Hottest 100 had been broadcast on 26 January, Australia Day, of the following year.

The Hottest 100 has a new home.

You heard right, our biggest music celebration of the year has a new date! On Saturday 27 January 2018 we'll be counting down the Hottest 100 songs of the year, as voted by you. Then, we'll back it up on Sunday with the songs that just missed out, the Hottest 200.

Welcome to the Hottest 100 Weekend. It's the countdown you love, made bigger!

Triple j is making this move after hearing directly from you. Heaps of you took part in our online survey as part of our review of the date of the Hottest 100. (You can read more about that process below.) You told us how much you love the countdown and most of you are up for a new day. We all agreed that the Hottest 100 shouldn't be part of a debate about the day it's on. The only debate should be about the songs ("Ya joking shoulda been higher").

Triple j will be freed up to celebrate Australia Day as its own event too. We have some new programming planned for 26 January (more on that later).

So, get your crew together and make sure you keep the 4th weekend in January free, 'cause the Hottest 100 Weekend is gonna be huge.

We're sure you've got tonnes of questions, so let's answer them.

What are the key dates for my diary?

Tues 12 Dec 2017: Voting opens
Mon 22 Jan 2018: Voting closes
Fri 26 Jan 2018: Australia Day
Sat 27 Jan 2018: Hottest 100
Sun 28 Jan 2018: Hottest 200

Why did you choose the fourth weekend of January?

We went with the fourth weekend of January because we wanted to keep all the best bits you love about the Hottest 100 – the music and being with your mates on a day that most people have off – and still host it at the same time in summer you're used to. It also means we can follow up that weekend with the 200-101 countdown.

Hasn't the Hottest 100 always been on 26 January?

No, the Hottest 100 has been held on a few different dates in the past so it's not the first time it's moved around. The first ever countdown was held on 5 March, 1989 and the countdown didn't regularly match up with 26 January until 1998. In fact, the 2004 countdown was on 25 January. So, the date of the countdown has moved around and though the Hottest 100 has mostly been held on Australia Day, it's not about Australia Day.

Why is the Hottest 100 moving?

It's fair to say there's been increasing debate around 26 January and there are a lot of perspectives on what it means to different Australians. As the public broadcaster representing all Australians, triple j and the ABC doesn't take a view in the discussions.

However, in recent years the Hottest 100 has become a symbol in the debate about Australia Day. The Hottest 100 wasn't created as an Australia Day celebration. It was created to celebrate your favourite songs of the past year. It should be an event that everyone can enjoy together – for both the musicians whose songs make it in and for everyone listening in Australia and around the world. This is really important to us.

Whether you're listening in Busselton, Bundy, Alice or Aspen. From Coober Pedy to Caz's pool, tuning in from a backyard BBQ or streaming from overseas, in the city or on the farm; everyone is invited to join the party.

What did people have to say about the date of the Hottest 100?

Your voice in this decision is as important as ours – you are the ones who listen, vote, and tune in so we wanted to hear from you. We've learnt all the way through that this is a complex issue and there have been a lot of different perspectives on what triple j should do. When we asked how you felt about triple j's Hottest 100 being held on January 26, we received tens of thousands of responses to our questionnaire – 64,990 responses to be precise.

An independent research company analysed a representative sample of these answers, from people of all walks of life, so we could better understand what you thought about the date of the Hottest 100. We learnt that the majority of you (60%) were in favour of moving the Hottest 100 to a different date.

For those that don't want the date to move, we have heard you. We've listened closely to how all of you felt about the Hottest 100 and responded with what's the right choice, right now, that reflects the variety of complicated views. And it's a move backed up by more than those survey results.

So, what is this year's #1 song going to be?

Well, that's over to you! Start getting your playlists sorted; voting for the 2018 Hottest 100 countdown opens Tuesday 12 December.

Source: triple j, 'triple j's Hottest 100 is moving to a new date and here's why', ABC, <https://www.abc.net.au/triplej/news/triple-j-hottest-100-is-moving-to-a-new-date-and-heres-why/9197254>, 27 November 2017

Section C: Sustained expository response

Instructions

- Section C requires a sustained expository response to one question.
- In your response, you are expected to:
  - » demonstrate your ability to use relevant, descriptive and appropriate metalanguage
  - » demonstrate familiarity with the topics of Unit 3, 'Language variation and purpose', and the topics of Unit 4, 'Language variation and identity'
  - » refer to the stimulus material provided.
- Each question is worth 30 marks.

Question 1 (30 marks)

'From social media to international media to the proliferation of online gaming, the Internet is clearly having an impact on language whether we like it or not.'

Discuss with reference to contemporary Australian society. Refer to at least **two** subsystems of language in your response.

Stimulus A

DM

NOUN (dms) *informal*

A private message sent on social media, especially Twitter.

VERB (dms, dming, dm'd, dmed) [WITH OBJECT] *informal*

Send (someone) a private message on social media, especially Twitter.

Origin Early 21st-century abbreviate of direct message, from the Direct Message feature of the social media application Twitter.

Adapted from *Oxford English Dictionary* by Oxford University Press. Accessed at Lexico.com. Reproduced with permission of the Licensor through PLSclear

Stimulus B

'... if my undergraduates are anything to go by, emojis are also a generational battleground. Like skinny jeans and side partings, the "laughing crying emoji", better known as 😂, fell into disrepute among the young in 2020 – just five years after being picked as the Oxford Dictionaries' 2015 Word of the Year. For gen Z TikTok users, clueless millennials are responsible for rendering many emojis utterly unusable – to the point that some in gen Z barely use emojis at all.'

Mark Brill (Birmingham City University), 'Apple's new emojis are more ammunition for the online generation wars', *The Conversation*, <https://theconversation.com/apples-new-emojis-are-more-ammunition-for-the-online-generation-wars-155974>, 26 February 2021

Stimulus C

'"Noob" is another very common term that is not only used in gaming but also on the internet in general. This term is used to describe a player who is new to the game or inexperienced. It's not necessarily an insult, but it can be used as one if someone is being rude. Players who use this term may be trying to show their experience in the game and assert their dominance. If someone calls you a "noob", don't take it too personally, and keep playing to improve.'

Stryda website, 'Gaming slang: How to talk like a pro gamer in 2023', <https://stryda.gg/news/gaming-slang-how-to-talk-like-a-pro-gamer-2023>, 14 April 2023

Stimulus D

'American English pervades our language 24/7 … We touch base. Reach out. At sidewalk cafes, we say wait up, my bad, no biggie. From the get-go, pissed meant drunk, but thanks to Yanks the label can now mean rankled (sorry, sore) as much as sozzled. The trend is annoying, period.'

David Astle, 'How *Succession* saved the English language', *The Sydney Morning Herald*, <https://www.smh.com.au/culture/books/how-succession-saved-the-english-language-20230717-p5dos9.html>, 18 July 2023

Question 2 (30 marks)

'Language has important societal purposes, and it fosters feelings of both group identity and solidarity.'

Discuss, referring to at least **two** subsystems of language in your response.

Stimulus A

'Billy always spoke a smattering of Gamilaraay words, but growing up Aboriginal in small town Collarenebri in north west NSW, "language was in some ways the most difficult thing to access."

"My mob were told you can't talk it, don't you dare speak that, even don't say you're Aboriginal, even that far."

Now 45, he's started formal lessons in Gamilaraay ... For Billy, speaking his language is about identity. "There's … a sense of connection," ... he explains.'

Masako Fukui, 'Australia has been called "a graveyard of languages". These people are bucking the trend' in 'Tongue Tied and Fluent', *Earshot*, ABC Radio National, 30 November 2019. Reproduced by permission of the Australian Broadcasting Corporation – Library Sales. Masako Fukui © 2019 ABC

Stimulus B

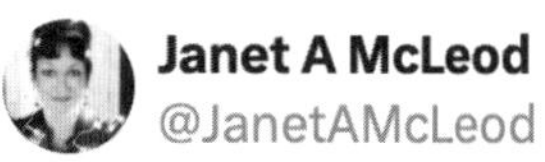

I've noticed a recent trend for Australian social media users to adopt the American informal second-person plural pronoun "y'all". Come on, Australia, we can do better. The correct term is "youse".

10:49 AM · Jan 19, 2021 from Melbourne, Victoria

Post on X (formerly known as Twitter)

Stimulus C

> 'This one fed was chatting about how hackers and that be trying to confuse u with some big politician type words to yoink ur info. Mans was tryna let u know that y'all Gen Z be no cap most likely to fall for the scammers trickery.'

Australian Federal Police Media Release, <https://www.afp.gov.au/news-centre/media-release/bestie-thats-not-slay-gen-z-more-likely-anyone-else-fall-victim>, 24 November 2023

Stimulus D

> 'There are two different kinds of accents. One is a "foreign" accent; this occurs when a person speaks one language using some of the rules or sounds of another one. For example, if a person has trouble pronouncing some of the sounds of a second language they're learning, they may substitute similar sounds that occur in their first language. This sounds wrong, or "foreign", to native speakers of the language.
>
> The other kind of accent is simply the way a group of people speak their native language. This is determined by where they live and what social groups they belong to.'

Betty Birner, 'Why do some people have an accent?', *Linguistic Society of America*, <https://www.linguisticsociety.org/content/why-do-some-people-have-accent>

Question 3 (30 marks)

'Australia is a multicultural country, but its inhabitants must conform to language norms in order to fit in.'

To what extent is this true in contemporary Australian society? Refer to at least **two** subsystems of language in your response.

Stimulus A

> 'We found many first-generation migrant parents are hesitant to pass on their first language to their children. This is because they believe a different language at home will give their children a foreign accent.'

Chloé Diskin-Holdaway (University of Melbourne) and Paola Escudero (Western Sydney University), 'Don't be afraid to pass your first language, and accent, to your kids. It could be their superpower', *The Conversation*, <https://theconversation.com/dont-be-afraid-to-pass-your-first-language-and-accent-to-your-kids-it-could-be-their-superpower-143093>, 8 February 2021

Stimulus B

> 'The series is, to quote a line in one of the episodes, "like deadly, like Blackfulla deadly, not like gammin [fake or pretend]" – a must watch!'

Bronwyn Carlson (Macquarie University), '*Preppers* is a deep reading of colonial violence – and a hilarious, must-watch Aussie TV comedy', *The Conversation*, <https://theconversation.com/preppers-is-a-deep-reading-of-colonial-violence-and-a-hilarious-must-watch-aussie-tv-comedy-170100>, 10 November 2021

Stimulus C

'When Suresh first moved to Melbourne, he often wondered if Aussies had a language of their own. He knew his English was on par with native speakers. But he began to question his ability to understand the language after one week in the Land Down Under. "You have to be attentive when you come to Australia because an entirely new word is created by abbreviating or lengthening it," added Suresh.

Originally from India, he describes a funny incident while waiting for a friend at his university's library lawn. An Aussie student, Harry, who walked past the library, spotted Suresh, and asked, "How ya going?"

Surprised that his friend was concerned about how he would make his way into town, Suresh answered, "I am walking there." Puzzled, Harry just smiled awkwardly and walked away.'

IDP International English Language Testing System, 'Understanding the Aussie slang', <https://ielts.com.au/>, March 2021

Stimulus D

99.9 WHHS-FM, X (formerly known as Twitter), <https://t.co/rFdGRXGfww>, 12 June 2019

Question 4 (30 marks)

'Australian English is changing, as it must. And these changes should be welcomed.'

To what extent is this true in contemporary Australia? Refer to at least **two** subsystems of language in your response.

Stimulus A

> 'The Governor in Council has officially approved the new name for Moreland City Council, with the change to Merri-bek published in the Victorian Government Gazette today.
>
> Mayor, Councillor Mark Riley said he was delighted that the Merri-bek name will soon be seen across the municipality.
>
> "Changing the name of our city to Merri-bek is reconciliation in action with Traditional Owners. I'm excited that we are close to formally introducing our new name," Cr Riley said.'

'Merri-bek name for Council approved', Merri-bek City Council, <https://www.merri-bek.vic.gov.au/my-council/news-and-publications/news/merri-bek-name-for-council-approved/>, 15 September 2022

Stimulus B

Stimulus C

'This #BlakFriday, shout out to Noongar Yamatji Koorie and Yolngu songman Bobby Bennell. Bobby has been singing since before he could speak, using music for Truth Telling and empowering our mob. His song "Feel" has been added to the FIRST Apple Music First Nations playlist. Have a listen, link in bio 💪'

Senator Lidia Thorpe, Instagram post, 11 Nov 2022

Stimulus D

'When Eleni tells her friend Luca about her *Yiayia*, he has no idea what she's talking about. That is until he realises he has one too – a grandmother! Only his is called *Nonna*. In fact, all their friends have a grandmother – the only difference is the special name they have for her.

What do you call your grandmother?'

Stella Stamatakis, *What's a Yiayia? A Book About Grandmothers*, Butter Fingers Books, 2018

Question 5 (30 marks)

'Informal language forms an integral part of the Australian national identity.'

Discuss, referring to at least **two** subsystems of language in your response.

Stimulus A

<https://munhwaexperience.wordpress.com/2015/02/15/guide-to-aussie-culture-yonk-and-zonk/>, 15 February 2015

Stimulus B

> 'It goes without saying that slanguage has always played a pivotal role in the Australian sense of self. ANU researcher Evan Kidd recently set out empirically something Australians have intuitively known for a long time – "using Australian slang increases your likeability among other Australians".'

Howard Manns (Monash University), 'Slanguage and "dinky di" Aussie talk in elections', *The Conversation*, <https://theconversation.com/slanguage-and-dinky-di-aussie-talk-in-elections-59967>, 30 June 2016

Stimulus C

> 'Budget airline Bonza opened the naming rights to their first plane to the Australian public and has chosen the most Aussie name ever.
>
> After much deliberation, Bonza's first Boeing 737 MAX will be named "Shazza".
>
> Bonza asked Australians to "let us nick their nicknames," compiling a shortlist of hundreds to choose from.'

The Project, 'New budget airline Bonza name first Australian plane "Shazza"', 10 Play, <https://10play.com.au/theproject/articles/new-budget-airline-bonza-name-first-australian-plane-shazza/tpa220829zrgfo>, 29 August 2022

Stimulus D

> 'An interesting Aboriginal English word is "deadly" which would translate as "really good or impressive" in standard English. It appears that this is a word which is spreading from Aboriginal English into general Australian usage, especially among young people (compare the way that the African American English word "bad" to describe something very good has spread into many other varieties of English).'

Diana Eades, 'Aboriginal English', <https://www.hawaii.edu/satocenter/langnet/definitions/aboriginal.html>, accessed 2 July 2024

Question 6 (30 marks)

'Euphemisms are necessary in both formal and informal contexts.'

To what extent does this apply to contemporary Australian society? Refer to at least **two** subsystems of language in your response.

Stimulus A

> 'I'm here to fulfil the diversity quota … Somewhere, someone is watching through their television right now going … "I just paid six grand for this television and it shows no colour" … It's a go at the industry who doesn't [care] about diversity.'

Osamah Sami at the Australian Academy of Cinema and Television Arts (AACTA) Awards, December 2017

Stimulus B

> 'In the second half of the 20th century, we came to accept that in certain cases we should avoid deliberately hurtful language. While many deride political correctness for going too far, its initial aim to establish non-hateful language was, and still is, admirable …
>
> A number of paraphrases allow us to avoid sensitive terms …
>
> Some of these terms can go too far and are effectively euphemisms because they sound overdone and excessively delicate …'

Roland Sussex (University of Queensland), 'From "demented" to "person with dementia": how and why the language of disability changed', *The Conversation*, https://theconversation.com/from-demented-to-person-with-dementia-how-and-why-the-language-of-disability-changed-85172, 7 December 2017

Stimulus C

> 'So how do we talk about the business of "growing old" if it's such a sensitive subject?
>
> The answer of course is euphemism … To throw some light on this particular taboo, we set about analyzing the naming practices of "aged care facilities" (itself a nice euphemism) in the Melbourne region …
>
> We collected names from 2013 and compared them to those that were around in 1987 …
>
> The 2013 sample showed a far greater range of euphemistic strategies compared to the 1987 sample … nearly a third (63%) of the institutional names omitted any reference to their actual function. Instead, they employed a wide selection of uplifting metaphors that suggested the facility had nothing to do with aged care at all.'

Kate Burridge and Réka Benczes, Monash University, boobookeducation.com.au, 2016

Stimulus D

Steve Greenberg, 1996

Question 7 (30 marks)

'To achieve social cohesion, it is more important to be polite and considerate than it is to speak freely.'

To what extent is this true in contemporary Australian society? Refer to at least **two** subsystems of language in your response.

Stimulus A

> 'People probably don't think twice about using sayings like "bringing home the bacon" or "beating a dead horse". However, vegans want everyone to stop using these offensive phrases. Instead, they are promoting a more "animal-friendly language" around children ... The phrases include an option for "beating a dead horse" ("feeding a fed horse") as well as "put all your eggs in one basket" ("put all your berries in one bowl"). They also suggest saying "spill the beans" instead of "letting the cat out of the bag".'

Nobelle Borines, 'Vegans want you to stop saying "bring home the bacon" because it's offensive', *EliteReaders*, <https://www.elitereaders.net/vegans-want-to-you-to-stop-saying-bringing-home-the-bacon-because-its-offensive/>, 6 December 2018

Stimulus B

> 'Anonymous communication is seen by many as a cornerstone of promoting freedom of speech, expression and privacy on the internet, but it can also be misused to control and abuse people.'

eSafety Commissioner, <https://www.esafety.gov.au>, accessed 21 December 2023

Stimulus C

'The Victorian Government is committed to equality for all Victorians. The Inclusive Language Guide was created to provide public servants with the right tools to communicate in our diverse work environments. Language has the power to empower individuals and strengthen relationships. Through issuing this Guide, the Victorian Government acknowledges and celebrates our differences.'

Martin Foley, Victorian Government Inclusive Language Guide webpage,
© Copyright State Government of Victoria. Licensed under Creative Commons 4.0,
<https://creativecommons.org/licenses/by/4.0/legalcode>

Stimulus D

'The meaning of the things we say is subjective, filtered through our unique worldviews and experiences. But language still has a very real power over us. Words can insult or encourage, smooth over misunderstandings or create rifts.'

Advice on effective communication in a handbook on public speaking

Question 8 (30 marks)

'Language change caused by technology has made it difficult to communicate effectively with each other.'

To what extent do you agree? Refer to at least **two** subsystems of language in your response.

Stimulus A

'A linguistic arms race is raging online – and it isn't clear who's winning.

On one side are social networks like Facebook, Instagram and TikTok. These sites have become better and better at identifying and removing language and content that violates their community standards.

Social media users are on the other side, and they've come up with coded terminology designed to evade algorithmic detection. These expressions are collectively referred to as "algospeak."

... To get past content filters, social media users are making use of coded language instead of the banned terms ... "Leg booty" is LGBTQ.'

Roger J. Kreuz (University of Memphis), 'What is "algospeak"? Inside the newest version of linguistic subterfuge', *The Conversation,* <https://theconversation.com/what-is-algospeak-inside-the-newest-version-of-linguistic-subterfuge-203460>, 13 April 2023

Stimulus B

'Language changes. When it does, some people will think that the new usage is "wrong" because they were speaking a perfectly serviceable Saxon-Norse pidgin before. They are wrong to think it is wrong, but any user of the language ought at least to know that there are people who, wrongly, think that to use "literally" to mean "not literally" is wrong. When language changes, it makes sense not to be at the cutting edge of irritating your readers or listeners.'

John Rentoul, 'I literally stand by the (mis)use of "literally"', *The Independent*, <https://www.independent.co.uk/voices/comment/i-literally-stand-by-the-misuse-of-literally-8763533.html>, 15 August 2013. Reproduced by permission of Independent Digital News & Media Ltd

Stimulus C

> 'Of course words have meanings – meanings distinct enough that we can set them down in print and confidently say that this is what most people mean when they say … Language works by agreement of the masses. It's the original people power – a word means something because enough people use it to mean that thing. By extension, if enough people start using a word in a different way, or ignoring a particular rule, then meanings and uses can change.'

Charlotte Buxton, 'When does "wrong" become "right"?', Oxford Dictionaries blog, <https://blog.oxforddictionaries.com/2013/02/08/when-does-wrong-become-right/>, 2013. Reproduced by permission of Oxford University Press

Stimulus D

Ron Barrett, <http://ronbarrettart.com>

Question 9 (30 marks)

'Jargon is unnecessarily complicated language used to impress, rather than to inform, your audience.'

To what extent do you agree? Refer to at least **two** subsystems of language in your response.

Stimulus A

'jargon

Pronunciation /ˈ**järgən**/ /ˈ**dʒɑrgən**/

NOUN

1 Special words or expressions that are used by a particular profession or group and are difficult for others to understand.

"legal jargon"

Late Middle English (originally in the sense "twittering, chattering", later "gibberish")'

Oxford English Dictionary by Oxford University Press. Accessed at <https://www.lexico.com/definition/jargon>. Reproduced with permission of the Licensor through PLSclear

Stimulus B

'Our business is infested with idiots who try to impress by using pretentious jargon.'

David Ogilvy (advertising executive)

Stimulus C

'Aortic root is mildly dilated. Aortic valve is stenotic. The valve is tricuspid. There is fine fluttering of the aortic cusps.'

Verbal echocardiogram report to patient

Stimulus D

Question 10 (30 marks)

'While seemingly open to language change and variation, we still judge others based on how they use language.'

Is this true in the context of contemporary Australian society? Refer to at least **two** subsystems of language in your response.

Stimulus A

> 'Ms Davis said holding the view that Aboriginal English was broken English, or slang, was not only incorrect but could have detrimental impacts on learning outcomes for Indigenous students ...
>
> "If kids are speaking Aboriginal English you might have different sounds, phonology, semantics and pragmatics that goes with it."
>
> Ms Davis said 80 per cent of Indigenous Australians were Aboriginal-English speakers and the way it was spoken varied based on different language groups.'

Madison Snow, 'Aboriginal English recognition in schools critical for improving student outcomes for Indigenous Australians', *ABC Goldfields*, December 2019. Reproduced by permission of the Australian Broadcasting Corporation – Library Sales. Madison Snow © 2019 ABC

Stimulus B

> 'Negative attitudes to **uptalk** are not new. In 1975, the linguist Robin Lakoff drew attention to the pattern in her book *Language and Women's Place*, which argued that women were socialized to talk in ways that lacked power, authority, and confidence.'

Richard Nordquist, 'Speech patterns: Uptalking', <https://www.thoughtco.com/uptalk-high-rising-terminal-1692574>, updated 8 March 2018

Stimulus C

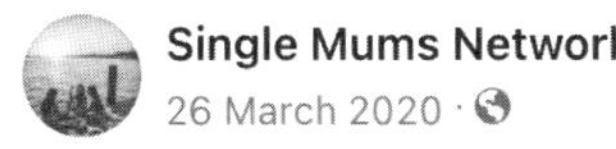

Putting on my best bogan Aussie accent! And can confirm since the recent announcement we are now 1.5m apart. Nothing like a cheeky rosè and your bestie on the porch!

Single Mums Network, Facebook, March 2020

Stimulus D

'If you're unsure what someone's pronoun is, you can ask them respectfully, and preferably privately. Use a question like "Can I ask what pronoun you use?" Do not ask "What pronoun do you prefer?" A person's pronoun and identity are not a preference. Instead, just ask what pronoun they use.'

'LGBTIQ+ Inclusive Language Guide', © Copyright State Government of Victoria, <https://www.vic.gov.au/inclusive-language-guide>. Licensed under Creative Commons 4.0, <https://creativecommons.org/licenses/by/4.0/legalcode>

Extra space for responses

Suggested responses

Section A: Short answer

Note that questions with 4–5 points available are often graded holistically. You can find the assessment criteria for all sections of the exam on the VCAA (Victorian Curriculum and Assessment Authority) webpage for English Language assessment, https://www.vcaa.vic.edu.au/assessment/vce-assessment/past-examinations/Pages/English-Language.aspx

TEXT A

Question 1

Sample response

> The speaker uses front focus to create cohesion in lines 1 to 5: 'When I was sixteen (1)', 'when I was thirty-one' (3), 'now I'm sixty-one' (5). The placement of an adverbial clause before each main clause draws attention to the passing of time as well as the connection between time and the change in the speaker's attitude.

Other answers might refer to front focus of subordinate clauses and/or adverbials (rather than adverbial clauses as per the above sample).

Mark allocation: 2 marks

- 1 mark for correctly identifying the front focus created by an adverbial/subordinate clause
- 1 mark for correctly identifying that the front focus creates or reinforces the connection between the passing of time and the speaker's attitude

Question 2

Sample response

> In Text 1, French uses a metaphor to refer to her age as 'the afternoon tea of life' (26) before going on to explain what she believes 'we afternoon tea-ers need to teach ... children' (27–28). Here, the metaphor highlights the experience and wisdom that senior Australians can offer by creating a semantic connection between ageing and the meal cycle of a single day. The metaphor suggests that because French has already enjoyed the day's earlier meals, she is in a position to give advice to those who have yet to experience any of them. In this way, French is able to establish herself as an authority whose beliefs about encouraging children to read should be adopted by her audience.

Other approaches

Other answers might refer to:

- the connection between the metaphors and other purposes or intents, such as sharing an ideological stance on reading
- the way the metaphor acts as a euphemism to make ageing seem more pleasant or attractive
- how 'heroes' (22) could be said to be used hyperbolically to facilitate the joke and build rapport with the listeners.

Mark allocation: 4 marks

- This question should be marked holistically, using the guide below.
  - 4 marks: The response demonstrates a detailed knowledge of the text and is supported by relevant examples/evidence. Metalanguage is used appropriately and effectively. Features of written discourse are consistently used.
  - 2 to 3 marks: The response demonstrates a sound knowledge of the text and is supported by some examples/evidence. The metalanguage used is relevant. Some features of written discourse are evident.
  - 0 to 1 mark: The response demonstrates a limited knowledge of the text and contains few examples. The use of metalanguage is limited or absent. Few features of written discourse are evident.

Question 3

Sample response

> The modal verbs function rhetorically in the text to enable the argument. The possibility in 'could change' (2) is contrasted with the stress on the greater certainty of 'can change' (11), persuading the audience that books will make the difference. In this, French also uses past tense in 'I thought' (2) to demonstrate her outdated thinking before moving into the present tense in her hypothetical 'if you want more intelligent children give them more books' (16–17). Here, the paralleled present tense verbs want/give suggest an immediately available solution and the simple tense emphasises the simplicity of the solution.

Mark allocation: 4 marks

- This question should be marked holistically, using the guide below.
  - 4 marks: The response demonstrates a detailed knowledge of the text and is supported by relevant examples/evidence. Metalanguage is used appropriately and effectively. Features of written discourse are consistently used.
  - 2 to 3 marks: The response demonstrates a sound knowledge of the text and is supported by some examples/evidence. The metalanguage used is relevant. Some features of written discourse are evident.
  - 0 to 1 mark: The response demonstrates a limited knowledge of the text and contains few examples. The use of metalanguage is limited or absent. Few features of written discourse are evident.

Question 4

Sample response

The text serves a conative function, encouraging listeners to promote reading in children. To achieve this, French establishes her authority to speak on the topic. She cites her age in 'now I'm sixty-one/' (5) and the rising intonation marks this as the reason for her authority, which is subsequently indicated by the falling intonation on the verb phrase 'I know\' (6). This creates an authoritative tenor so that when French smiles when she utters her central claim 'a book can change the world' in line 12, the smile is encouraging to the audience, empowering them to follow her advice, achieving the conative function.

French further achieves a conative function through the use of stress on the adverb 'every' (13), the adjective 'intelligent' (14) and the noun phrase 'more books' (17). The rhythm of these emphasised words establishes a semantic link between them, reinforcing the importance of books for children. At the end of her speech, French uses a gesture, holding her hand out (32) to demonstrate her words 'to hold our hands out' (32), indicating that she is including the audience in her instruction. Thus, the audience is personally instructed to 'say yes' (32) in the subsequent imperative phrase, achieving the conative function.

Other approaches: French uses both tempo and pausing to engage her listeners, for example in the use of humour in lines 20–23 which builds rapport with the audience, indicated by the applause in line 24.

Mark allocation: 5 marks

- This question should be marked holistically, using the guide below.
  - 4 to 5 marks: The response demonstrates a detailed knowledge of the text and is supported by relevant examples/evidence. Metalanguage is used appropriately and effectively. Features of written discourse are consistently used.
  - 2 to 3 marks: The response demonstrates a sound knowledge of the text and is supported by some examples/evidence. The metalanguage used is relevant. Some features of written discourse are evident.
  - 0 to 1 mark: The response demonstrates a limited knowledge of the text and contains few examples. The use of metalanguage is limited or absent. Few features of written discourse are evident.

TEXT B

Question 1

Sample response

> The syntactic pattern of listing is used between lines 1 and 5, with McGowan listing the areas of his constituency as 'Eltham, Montmorency, Greensborough ... Eltham North' to alert his audience to their residence in his electorate, given they will know their suburb but may not know their electorate.

Other approaches: Another syntactic pattern you may refer to in your response is parallelism: 'no new car parks, no new station' (lines 14–15) gives a sense of growing exclusion, or 'a vote for me in November is a vote for CRITICAL rail duplication' (line 16), implying that voters will personally benefit.

Mark allocation: 2 marks

- 1 mark for both labelling the type of pattern (listing, parallelism, antithesis) and accurately quoting an example
- 1 mark for giving a reason for the use of this pattern

TIPS

» **You must ensure that you label the type of syntactic pattern. No marks will be awarded if the type of syntactic pattern is not labelled. Thus, the answer 'The syntactic pattern used between lines 1 and 5, of "Eltham, Montmorency, Greensborough ... Eltham North"' would not garner marks.**

» **Don't overdo the answer. You have only been given a few lines of space and it is only worth 2 marks.**

Question 2

Sample response

> The suburb of Montmorency is referred to in a shortened form with a hypocoristic suffix: 'Monty' in lines 9 and 14. This colloquial name builds rapport between the candidate and his voters by implying a shared prior knowledge of this affectionate diminutive.

Other approaches: Other acceptable answers may refer to the use of capitals for emphasis in the adverb 'NOT' (8), adjective 'CRITICAL' (16) and adverb 'IMPORTANTLY' (17) and their role in the intention to win votes; or the colloquialism '100%' in line 20, which addresses the purpose of building trustworthiness.

Mark allocation: 2 marks

- 1 mark for accurately identifying an element of informal language
- 1 mark for linking this to a relevant purpose or intent

TIPS

» **Avoid contractions as an example of informal language. Firstly, they can be used formally – particularly in spoken mode – and secondly, they rarely offer much material for interesting analysis.**

» **You must use specific evidence to demonstrate your opinion on the purpose with reference to line numbers.**

» **It is important to use accurate metalanguage.**

Question 3

Sample response

Passive voice is used in the following examples: 'must be addressed' (6–7), 'if re-elected' (8–9) and 'will be forced' (9). The passive in lines 6–7 ('must be addressed') is agentless; the implied agent is McGowan and his party, and the reader infers that the Liberal Party will immediately address 'traffic congestion' (6) if elected. This is followed by a second agentless passive in lines 8–9 ('if re-elected'), where the reader infers that agents who may potentially re-elect Daniel Andrews are the people being addressed by McGowan in the letter. This implies that only McGowan's party can address traffic congestion, as the Labor Party has refused to do so. Finally, the Labor Party is the implied agent of the agentless passive in line 9 ('will be forced'); by refusing to address the problem of traffic congestion by increasing rail services, they are responsible for any inconvenience to 'Eltham and Monty station commuters' (9).

Mark allocation: 4 marks

- 1 mark for identifying the uses of passive voice in the relevant lines (all three instances must be identified)
- 3 marks for accurate analysis of each use of passive voice, using evidence and appropriate metalanguage

TIPS

» Unless a specific number of examples are requested, when a question asks you to comment on the use of a language feature between a set of lines, it is important that you identify and comment on every instance of that language feature contained within these parameters.

» Pay attention to the number of marks a question is worth to determine how detailed your analysis should be.

» Ensure you use accurate and complete metalanguage, such as 'agentless passive'.

Question 4

Sample response

McGowan's identity as a passionate and dedicated candidate for election is demonstrated in his campaign letter. His capitalisation of the adverb 'NOT' in line 8 implies a sense of outrage at the perceived disservice Labor will deliver to the area if re-elected, demonstrating his commitment to addressing traffic congestion. This is further reinforced by similar capitalisation of the adjective 'CRITICAL' (16), which implies that Labor has been less concerned about the rail upgrades than McGowan will be, if elected.

McGowan's identity as an Australian as well as a 'local' of the area in which his campaign is running is demonstrated through his use of the hypocoristic suffix in 'Monty' (9, 14); this is a term commonly used by Montmorency locals as a substitution for the suburb name. As the hypocoristic use of suffixes is a common feature of Australian English, the use of 'Monty' serves to highlight the authenticity of McGowan's Australian identity.

Mark allocation: 3 marks

- 2 marks for discussion of language features that reflect McGowan's identity
- 1 mark for appropriate use of metalanguage

TIP

» It is okay to repeat evidence across questions in the Short Answer Questions, so long as the evidence is relevant in both cases – as in the sample response in Q2 and Q4. Ensure that the evidence is in fact relevant and remember that you should **not** do this for Analytical Commentaries.

Question 5

Sample response

Formatting

The use of varying fonts and bolding contributes to the coherence of the text. The initial imperative with the listing of suburbs ('Save ... Eltham North') has been printed in three different font sizes, with three suburbs much larger than the others. This implies that 'Eltham, Montmorency, Greensborough' (2–3) will be the focus of the campaign letter even though it is addressed to the residents of all listed suburbs. Similarly, the citation about Labor's plans to 'reduce the number of car parks at Greensborough station' (12–13) in lines 23–24 is in a smaller font than the rest of the text. This aids coherence as it implies that this is additional information given as a reference rather than part of McGowan's core campaign message.

McGowan has used selective bolding to highlight his core campaign message. This can be seen in the bolded declarative sentence in line 20: 'I am 100% committed ...'. Further, he capitalises select lexemes in the text, such as the adjective 'CRITICAL' (16), the adverb 'IMPORTANTLY' (17) and the noun 'RAIL' (20), to highlight his party's opinion as to the necessity of the changes they are proposing to reduce congestion.

Inference

Readers can infer that McGowan is a local member of the area in which he is campaigning through the use of inclusive personal pronouns such as 'our' (6, 8). McGowan's comment that 'Daniel Andrews' (8) will not 'duplicate our rail to Eltham station' (8) allows readers to infer that Andrews does not care about 'Eltham and Monty station commuters' (9).

The use of the passive voice in '[congestion] must be addressed' (6–7) implies that if readers vote for McGowan, he will address traffic congestion but re-electing Labor will mean it is not addressed.

Mark allocation: 4 marks

- This question should be marked holistically, using the guide below.
  - 4 marks: The response demonstrates a detailed knowledge of factors contributing to coherence and is supported by relevant examples/evidence from the text. Metalanguage is used appropriately and effectively. Features of written discourse are consistently used.
  - 2 to 3 marks: The response demonstrates a sound knowledge of factors contributing to coherence and is supported by some examples/evidence from the text. The metalanguage used is relevant. Some features of written discourse are evident.
  - 0 to 1 mark: The response demonstrates a limited knowledge of the factors contributing to coherence and contains few examples from the text. The use of metalanguage is limited or absent. Few features of written discourse are evident.

TIPS

- When discussing inference, ensure you explain fully what is inferred by the reader; to score highly, your response must do more than simply state that a reader must 'know' about an element to understand it.
- Inference is not the same as prior knowledge. You cannot infer from this text that Eltham is a suburb of Melbourne – this is prior knowledge. You can infer that the suburbs listed in lines 4–5 all fall into McGowan's electorate.
- Pay attention to the instruction term in the question – in this case, 'analyse'. This indicates that you must do more than simply provide a list of examples to produce a high-scoring response. You must analyse the coherence of the text with reference to its context and purpose.
- That being said, it would be difficult to achieve full marks if only one or two examples were explained, or if the examples chosen were inappropriate. Read the text carefully and select the most pertinent examples of the relevant language features to support your argument.

TEXT C

Question 1

Sample response

Alcott's use of emphatic stress for the adverbial phrase 'all four' (24) and elongated vowel sound in the adverb 'a=ll' (26) highlights the impressive nature of winning multiple grand slams.

Alcott uses a fast tempo on line 16, '<A Actually it was quite funny, A>', which functions to quickly flag the value of the forthcoming anecdote as 'funny' before moving into the content of the anecdote about his dad (17–20), which is the focus of his answer so normally paced.

Other approaches

Other prosodic features in this section of the dialogue include:

- rising pitch, which serves varied functions such as to pass the floor (33)
- falling pitch to indicate the end of that anecdote before moving to the next point (22).

Mark allocation: 3 marks

- 1 mark for each prosodic feature identified, with accurate comments on how each feature functions specifically in this text, avoiding generic responses (up to 3 marks)

TIPS

» **This question requires knowledge of the prosodic features, which are intonation, pitch, stress, tempo and volume. Do not confuse vocal effects such as laughter or an intake of breath with prosodic features.**

» **In your response, include transcription symbols that are relevant to your analysis.**

» **Avoid generic responses like 'the fast tempo quickly moves onto the more important part' – this does not explain why one part of the utterance is more important than the other.**

Question 2

Sample response

A friendly tenor reflects the roles of the participants as interviewer and interviewee. In these roles, there is a need for them to simulate a sense of closeness and familiarity, which serves to give the audience the impression that the interviewer knows Alcott well. Steinfort uses an informal and playful register in the fragment sentence in line 2, with ellipsis of the subject and including only the noun phrase 'decent night of partying' (2) when he asks the quite intimate question of whether Alcott has been drinking alcohol – euphemistically described as 'partying'. Steinfort continues this informal register when he shifts topic, with an interrogative that begins with an informal discourse marker 'yeah' in 'yeah what is it, nine grand slam ... titles now?' (13–14). As the topics become more professional – celebrities, Alcott's career and legacy – the tenor regains some distance and the register becomes more formal, evidenced in Steinfort's final question on line 63: 'Why do you think people have embraced it so much', which uses positive politeness and a Standard formation to seek Alcott's opinion.

Mark allocation: 3 marks

- 1 mark for identifying the tenor
- 2 marks for linking this to an accurate register using examples

TIPS

» **This question requires a description of the register which includes both formality and style.**

» **Note that the examples used here are all about the questions asked by the interviewer. This gives the answer structure and avoids rambling or disjointed responses. This is a useful focus because questions are the point at which the interaction occurs and the tenor is most obvious.**

Question 3

Sample response

The semantic field in the opening of the interview relates to Alcott's 'partying' (2). Given the situational context of an early morning interview after Alcott's winning tournament, his celebratory drinking is addressed. This is somewhat taboo in the situational context of daytime television, so the interlocutors use euphemisms such as the adjectival complements 'a bit average' (3) and 'a bit dusty' (10), which are both metaphorical ways to express that Alcott is feeling ill from too much alcohol. The *Today Show* uses a video clip to end this section and introduce the second semantic field of tennis, for which Alcott is known. This includes collocations such as 'grand slam' (14) and the proper noun 'Wimbledon' (17), which is synonymous with the tennis competition that is held at the stadium of the same name.

Other approaches

Other answers might consider:

- the semantic field of celebrity (27–49), discussing lexicology including 'hero' (28) and 'hobnobbing' (33), or referring to syntax – 'there would be 10 people there' (41) and 'now there's packed stadiums' (43)
- how the final section (50–89) could be seen to focus on the semantic field of legacy (phonology and syntax in 'I just wanna lea=ve the sport in a better spot for the next generation of young athletes', 51), discussing how this segues into the field of hard work using semantics – 'train our backsides off' (66), 'warm fuzzy feeling' (72).

Mark allocation: 4 marks

- This question should be marked holistically, using the guide below.
  - 3 to 4 marks: The response identifies two semantic fields and discusses each, with reference to how they are linked to each other. This is supported by relevant examples/evidence from the text. Metalanguage is used appropriately and effectively and is drawn from at least two different subsystems.
  - 2 marks: The response demonstrates a sound knowledge of the semantic fields but does not sufficiently explore the connections between them OR does not include examples. Some relevant metalanguage is used, drawn from two subsystems of language.
  - 0 to 1 mark: The response demonstrates limited knowledge of the semantic fields and contains few or no examples from the text. The use of metalanguage is limited or absent or not drawn from two different subsystems of language.

TIP

» **Note the necessity of discussing two subsystems of language. This means that you need to label your examples with metalanguage that references features from at least two of: phonetics and phonology, morphology, lexicology, syntax, discourse and pragmatics, and semantics.**

Question 4

Sample response

Alcott's use of Australian English is reflected through his use of a laid-back and informal register. He uses the popular Australian vocative noun 'ma=te' (3) in his response to Steinfort's first interrogative of the interview, elongating the vowel sound to build the shared connection about the results of 'partying' (2). Furthermore, Alcott hedges his discussion of his emotions, using the adverb 'a bit' (8), the figurative euphemism 'I let ... it all out' (9) and collocation 'warm fuzzy feeling' (72) to convey his feelings without losing face given it is the nature of many Australians to be emotionally reserved.

Alcott also uses the idiomatic phrases 'that guy kicks' (82) and 'train our backsides off' (66), assuming his Australian audience will understand his meaning, as it reflects their value of hard work leading to success.

The Australian accent is also in evidence. The word final [g] is elided from 'feelin' (10), as is the [d] in 'an' (54). Furthermore, the [l] in 'Australian' is assimilated in Alcott's pronunciation to 'Austrayan' (44, 86), reflecting the relaxed pronunciation that keeps the tongue low in the mouth.

Other approaches

Other features of Australian English include:

- the use of humour when Alcott uses declaratives to tell the story about his dad (17–20), which is subtly critical of him
- the discourse particle 'like' (37, 65) and hyperbolic language 'awesome' (55) and 'he dominates' (84), typical of a younger Australian such as Alcott
- Australian colloquialisms 'get around you' (86) and 'feelin' a bit dusty' (10)
- phrases such as 'really means a lot' (49), 'really makes me feel good' (85) and 'really honoured' (88), with the adverb 'really' intensifying each sentiment, showing passion and commitment.

Mark allocation: 5 marks

- This question should be marked holistically, using the guide below.
  - 4 to 5 marks: The response identifies a range of features of Australian English and shows excellent understanding of the context.
  - 2 to 3 marks: The response identifies two or more features of Australian English and shows some awareness of the context.
  - 0 to 1 mark: The response identifies a feature of Australian English but there is no awareness of context.

TIPS

- **Pay attention to the number of marks to determine how detailed the analysis should be.**
- **Ensure you label examples with metalanguage and provide line numbers in your response.**
- **This type of question can be used as a discriminator as it requires an appropriate number of examples from the text and a high level of detail.**

TEXT D

Question 1

Sample response

> The register of the text is upbeat and informal. The affectionate textspeak nouns 'doggos' and 'puppers' in line 27 reflect this register, building a closer social distance with an audience of pet owners who are likely to use this language themselves.

Other approaches

Other language features that contribute to an upbeat and informal register include:

- opening 'Hi' (3) uses features of the spoken mode to reduce formality
- exclamative 'Yay!' (6) uses features of the spoken mode to create excitement
- pronouns 'we're' (4) and 'you' (7) suggests a shared community within the neighbourhood
- ellipsis of subject in the interrogative 'Sound good?' (16) uses features of the spoken mode to reduce formality
- initialisms 'DIY' (14) and 'BYO' (23) celebrate the shared interests within the community of neighbours.

The register of this text is informal however you could refer to it with a modifier such as 'mostly'. There are formal elements; however, it is not a formal text as it is from a social group on a mobile/internet application. To strengthen your answer, qualify the style of the text as well, as this will demonstrate further insight. Other appropriate adjectives might include 'engaged', 'informative', or 'inclusive'. Be sure to select evidence that suits your description.

Mark allocation: 2 marks

- 1 mark for accurately identifying the register and providing an appropriate example to support this description
- 1 mark for analysing the example in relation to the register

TIP

» **Use appropriate metalanguage from the Study Design in your response. Terms such as 'short words' would not be sufficient when labelling a language feature that supports an informal register.**

Question 2

Sample response

The situational context is a written social media post that uses a warm and welcoming tenor to inform the community about upcoming events in their area. As such, the formatting uses bolded headings (1, 9, 19 and 33) to orient readers to information that is relevant to them, like residing in the setting highlighted by the noun phrase 'Alphington Neighbourhood' (1) or wanting to attend a 'Christmas party' (19), which is from the semantic field of 'events'. This allows them to locate relevant information efficiently.

Other approaches

- Inference from the field of 'events': given the type of event and the modal verb in 'no profit will be made' (24), readers could infer that they should not try to sell anything.
- Logical ordering related to the setting: for example, the first paragraph makes the target audience of 'Alphington residents' explicit so readers know if it is relevant to themselves.
- Consistency and convention affecting the tenor: a comments section at the end of the post (33–42) encourages community engagement to create a welcoming tenor.

Mark allocation: 3 marks

- 1 mark for accurately identifying the situational context of the text
- 2 marks for providing an explanation of how an accurately labelled feature of coherence reflects the context identified

TIPS

» The features of situational context are tenor, text type, setting, field and mode. Note that, as in the sample response, these can be collated into a description. In this text, the tenor with the community is warm and welcoming (you could use other descriptors such as participatory or friendly); the text type is a social media post with a written mode; the field is upcoming events; and the setting is the audience's neighbourhood and the online space to which the text is posted.

» The features of coherence are cohesion, inference, logical ordering, formatting, consistency and conventions. You must use one of these five terms, even if your example is more specific than this. In the sample response, bolding, as an element of formatting, is considered.

» Although cohesion is an element of coherence, students struggle to discuss how an element of cohesion impacts coherence itself. If you're unsure, focus on the other four aspects of coherence instead.

Question 3

Sample response

> Technology has influenced the innovative use of language, such as the textspeak nouns 'doggos' and 'puppers' in line 27. Furthermore, the comment on line 38 uses a smiling emoji to add a tone of appreciation to 'Great initiative'. The influence of social media technology is reflected in the conversational style of the text, which imitates the spoken mode, as in the exclamative 'Yay!' in line 6 and the spelling of the verb 'looooooves' (40) which imitates the elongation of the vowel sound in a spoken mode. These examples project a sense of friendliness and approachability from community members as they aim to participate, and inspire others to participate, both in the forum and in neighbourhood social events.

Other approaches

Other examples that are valid for this question include:

- The declarative sentence on line 8 starts with the coordinating conjunction 'And'.
- The adjective 'FREE!' (line 8) and the collocation 'SAVE THE DATE!' (which is also underlined; line 42) are all in capitals, which generally indicates a loud volume and/or emphatic stress.
- The emojis in line 31 convey a cool and fun attitude.

Mark allocation: 3 marks

- 1 mark for accurately identifying features that are influenced by technology and including quotes with line numbers
- 1 mark for providing reasonable explanations of why the features have been used – this could be linked to text type, identity or purpose
- 1 mark for accurately using metalanguage

TIPS

» **The sample answer is longer than it needs to be, but for three marks, it is still worth discussing a couple of examples.**

» **Ensure your answer has a 'so what?' aspect. This means that you have gone beyond listing the influence of technology and added an explanation about why your example is being used or how it is impacting the text.**

Question 4

Sample response

John N.'s comment serves a phatic function by expressing 'thanks' (35) to the organisers, which is echoed by Anna Chew in the noun phrase 'Great initiative' (38). However, John's comment is also referential as he implies he will attend the event using a declarative 'Looking forward to Saturday' (35). Dhruv is likewise referential when he makes his attendance explicit: 'Will definitely attend' (40). This information alerts others to their intentions, which might influence the audience to also commit to attending. Mo A's comment is conative, using the imperative 'SAVE THE DATE' (42), which they follow up with a referential function as they offer information about the further upcoming event. Together the comments address the phatic function of building community.

Other approaches

Other examples that are valid for this question include:

- poetic function: emoji (38) or nonstandard spelling (40)
- emotive function: conveying excitement in the exclamation marks (35, 40 or 42).

Mark allocation: 3 marks

- In order to compare, at least two functions need to be identified, with one example for each. 1 mark for each accurately labelled function with an example and 1 mark for the comparison.
- To get full marks your answer must accurately discuss the functions and consider how they are used similarly or differently in the four comments.
- All examples should be labelled with metalanguage and line numbers provided.

TIP

» **Pay attention to the number of marks a question is worth and the number of lines provided to determine how detailed the analysis should be.**

Question 5

Sample response

The text's purpose is to give the community information about the community group and upcoming events. To achieve this purpose, a range of cohesive devices are used. Firstly, substitution is used: once the group is established as the semantic field in a lengthy noun phrase in line 4 starting with 'a local networking group', thereafter it is substituted with the shorter noun phrase 'the group' in line 5 and 7.

The values of the group are established using synonymy. They use a declarative sentence that lists positive outcomes of a community that is 'happier and more connected' (5–6). They also encourage participation by suggesting community members bring pets, which are described colloquially as 'doggos and puppers' (27). The authors close their post with a hope for a 'safe and happy' (29) summer. These examples of synonymy contribute to overall cohesion by setting a warm and welcoming tone. This is further achieved through the repetition of the coordinating conjunction 'and' in lines 25–26, which creates a list of the values held by the group.

A contrastive conjunction is used to fulfil the informative purpose of the text in 'but' (22), which is followed by a series of collocations regarding things the community should bring, including a 'picnic rug' (22), 'camp chairs' (22), and 'food and drinks' (23). The collocations simplify the information for readers and improve memorability for when they are planning their attendance.

The authors encourage community participation through a further collocation 'look forward' (29) and in the use of deictics in directing people to join the group through the 'link below' (7).

Mark allocation: 4 marks

- For a question like this, marking is holistic.
- As it is worth four marks, you should provide two to three features of cohesion in your response.
- Your features must include examples, line numbers and accurate metalanguage.
- It is important to choose relevant features when responding to this question. For full marks, you must engage with the given text and consider how the features of cohesion make this specific text cohesive. If you use generic explanations (see the tip below), it is unlikely that your answer will receive full marks.

TIPS

» **In Section A, examples from prior questions can be re-used. As long as the examples are accurate, this is acceptable in the exam.**

» **Features of cohesion are: lexical choice including synonymy, antonymy, hyponymy and hypernymy; collocation; information flow including clefting, front focus and end focus; anaphoric and cataphoric reference; deictics; repetition; ellipsis; substitution; conjunctions and adverbials.**

» **An example of a generic explanation is 'The use of deictics directs people to join the group through the "link below"' (7). This is exactly the same as the sample answer except that it leaves out 'The authors encourage community participation'. Without the mention of community as an outcome of cohesion, the example is just a definition and this will not garner strong marks.**

TEXT E

Question 1

Sample response

> On line 44, Ahana uses rising pitch at the end of her utterance to indicate she has more to say and is not ready to pass the floor yet.

Other approaches

Other possible responses include:

- pitch: falling pitch ('intonation' would be acceptable as well) indicates ceding the floor due to the overlap (53)
- intonation: continuing intonation indicates Ahana is not ready to pass the floor (52)
- tempo: fast tempo is used by Ahana to imitate the way she uttered the speech when she was trying to move on to the next topic with her partner, Ross (50)
- stress: Ahana's emphatic stress on the adverb 'really' and adjective 'insane' (51) emphasises that Ross thought the cost of the bottles was too much.

Mark allocation: 2 marks

- 1 mark for accurately identifying a prosodic feature
- 1 mark for discussing a function of the identified prosodic feature

TIPS

- » Ensure you do not comment on other discourse features such as the pause on line 51 and the overlaps – these are not prosodic features.
- » Avoid vague discussions of function such as 'the use of stress makes it stand out'. This would not be awarded full marks as this could be said of any example of stress! There must be clear links to the text or context of the given text.
- » Note that you are being asked for the function of a specific feature. In this instance, you do not need to refer to Jakobson's functions. Jakobson's functions occur at a discourse level.
- » Always use the metalanguage from the Study Design: for example, 'tempo' is correct so don't say 'pace'. You can still receive marks for an accurate explanation of the function of the feature, but you won't get full marks without the use of accurate metalanguage.

Question 2

Sample response

Lin takes the floor again on line 58 with the minimal response 'mmm', followed by the discourse marker 'so', before she loops back to the topic of her water bottle's value.

Other approaches

Other possible responses include:

- Melinda self-selects in response to Lin's use of final intonation on line 63. This provides opportunity for Melinda to topic-shift to how she damaged her own bottle (64).
- Ahana takes the floor using a pause filler, 'um' (70), as a hedge in order to shift the topic to a discussion about one of her girlfriends.
- On line 92, Lin shifts the topic to her partner's friend who makes apps. Ahana indicates on line 90 that she is ready to cede the floor through the use of final intonation, so Lin begins this new topic with a declarative.

Mark allocation: 2 marks

- 1 mark for accurately identifying an example of turn-taking
- 1 mark for appropriate discussion that includes metalanguage

TIP

» **When analysing topic changes or shifts, demonstrate your engagement with the text by clearly identifying the topics being discussed.**

Question 3

Sample response

One of the purposes of this text is for Lin, Ahana and Melinda to maintain rapport as they have a close relationship. In order to do this, all of the participants in this conversation adhere to an informal and friendly register. Casual lexical choices such as the interjection 'yep' (3, 4) and colloquial verb phrase 'gonna' (9), which has undergone elision and vowel reduction, show that they share a close social distance as they are comfortable using this informal language with each other.

Other approaches

Other purposes or intents that are supported by an informal register include:

- creating a sense of in-group membership based on the fact that these friends have the same water bottle
- meeting each other's positive face needs in order to maintain their friendship.

Other language features that support an informal and friendly register:

- Overlapping speech indicates that the conversation is unplanned and that the interlocutors have a close relationship. The interruptions do not threaten the others' face needs but instead indicate that the interrupter is listening and is interested.
- Discourse markers such as 'like' (12, 23, 33 etc.) indicate the relaxed context in which this conversation is taking place.
- The vocal effect of laughter is used throughout, which is informal as it helps to reduce social distance and shows that there is humour in the anecdotes.
- The coordinating conjunction 'and' is used to connect long anecdotes that are expressed in the form of declarative sentences (43–53). This shows the conversation is unplanned and that Ahana is thinking on the spot and using the conjunction to add information.

Mark allocation: 3 marks

- 1 mark for identifying the register as informal and friendly
- 1 mark for linking the register to an appropriate purpose or intent
- 1 mark for linking at least one discourse or language feature to the informal register of the text

TIP

» **Although this is worth three marks, the question is clear that you only need to discuss one feature to support your response. This is because you also need to accurately identify the register and a purpose. For this reason, don't overdo it! Simple will be effective here.**

Question 4

Sample response

On line 35, Lin poses the potentially threatening interrogative, 'How much was yours?', which could be seen as a threat to Melinda's negative face needs because of the taboo nature of discussion about money. Lin negotiates the threat through her use of laughter on line 37 and the declarative that acknowledges the interrogative might be perceived as 'rude'.

Mark allocation: 3 marks

- 1 mark for identifying the face-threatening act
- 1 mark for a valid explanation of how the act was negotiated by Lin
- 1 mark for including accurate line numbers and metalanguage

TIP

» **Being able to identify a face-threatening act that is a threat to positive or negative face needs shows you have a strong understanding of Brown and Levinson's theory of politeness.**

Question 5

Sample response

Ahana, Lin and Melinda share a close social distance and friendly tenor. They belong to a group for whom quality water bottles and value for money are markers of their group identity. This is apparent as they all contribute to the conversation about the topic of insulated water bottles. Question-and-answer adjacency pairs ensure that the conversation flows: for example, Lin invites Melinda to respond by posing the interrogative, 'is that a (.) one of those insulated water bottles?' on line 2. They are also comfortable interrupting each other with cooperative overlapping speech, such as when Ahana speaks over Lin by responding with '[No=]' on line 14. Minimal responses such as '[Oooooo/]' on line 18 show Melinda is interested in what Lin is saying about the colour of her water bottle, and regular laughter (83–85) builds their rapport, helping to establish a shared identity as money-conscious as they discuss the value of the water bottle. Familiarity is further indicated through prior knowledge when Lin and Ahana refer to their partners by their first names, 'James' (32) and 'Ross' (43), without having to explain who they are.

The main topic manager is Lin, as she introduces the subject of water bottles on line 1 and returns to the topic of the value of her water bottle on line 58 with the minimal response 'mmm' followed by the discourse marker 'so' to resume her story. Ahana and Lin are the dominant speakers as they hold the floor throughout most of the conversation, whereas Melinda's role is mostly to be an active listener who reacts to what the other two are saying, interjecting with phrases such as 'Yep' (3), '[No=]' (25) and laughter before 'nah nah' (38). The elongated vowel in the '[No=]' on line 25 further indicates she is engaged by what is being said.

Other approaches: The text maintains a close tenor as a result of the participants' equal power status as work colleagues, which creates a close social distance, and means that the function of their conversation is largely phatic. There are also elements of playfulness in this, seen in lines 86–87 with use of 'we' and the implication of a shared goal of retiring. There is supportive back-channelling, regular laughter and familiarity through inference that also contributes to a feeling of equal status, alongside cooperative overlap.

Mark allocation: 5 marks

- The 5 marks should be awarded holistically. The discussion should include at least three features of the discourse or language. Students should receive marks in the low/low–medium range (1–2) if they discuss discourse or language features but do not link them to the tenor or the group identity. To score highly, students must select relevant discourse and language features and link these to the tenor and group identity. High-scoring responses will show that the student can engage with the text in their response (for example, by using the information provided in the context description). In order to get full marks, all speakers must be discussed.
  - 4 to 5 marks: Demonstrates detailed knowledge and is supported by relevant examples/evidence from the text. Metalanguage is used appropriately and effectively. Features of written discourse are consistently used.
  - 2 to 3 marks: Demonstrates sound knowledge and is supported by some examples/evidence from the text. The metalanguage used is relevant. Some features of written discourse are evident.
  - 0 to 1 mark: Demonstrates limited knowledge and contains few examples from the text. The use of metalanguage is limited or absent. Few features of written discourse are evident.

TIP

» **There is a lot going on in this question. It is worth allowing a moment to re-read and check you have covered everything.**

TEXT F

Question 1

Sample response

One function of the text is referential: it uses headings and informative detail to give ticketholders information about using their tickets to get into the event. For example, the declarative sentence on line 9, 'All tickets are DIGITAL', is a heading that is followed by the location of the ticket as available in the 'app' (11) or through a 'web browser' (11). The options target the information for those who have the app and those who need to search via the web address, thus addressing the referential function.

Other approaches

Other possible functions and examples could include:

- conative: 'Be smarter than that and use the app instead' (22)
- poetic: 'It'll be – Delightful – for the environment if you don't print your tickets' (24)
- emotive: 'Hector would be proud of you' (26)
- phatic: 'Congrats! With patience, and maybe some tears' (3)

Mark allocation: 3 marks

- 1 mark for accurately identifying a function with an appropriate example
- 2 marks for discussing how that function is addressed by the example, using accurate and appropriate metalanguage

TIP

» **Except metalinguistic, any of the functions could be addressed. The trick is ensuring that the example you give and the explanation you offer does indeed address the function you identify. Conceivably, 'Congrats! With patience, and maybe some tears' (3) could be poetic or phatic so your justification needs to be plausible.**

Question 2

Sample response

Ticketmaster attempts to reduce the social distance and build rapport with ticketholders by using humour. In line 5, the author assumes that ticketholders have been 'fantasising'. This verb has connotations of fan obsession that could resonate with the target audience's identity and make them feel amused that a ticketing company knows their behaviour. This is further supported on line 8 with the lexical ambiguity of 'Hector's House', which simultaneously means the show and the album, and also titillatingly suggests Ticketmaster is letting the audience into Hector's home – a large reduction in social distance and a rapport-building fantasy for fans.

Other approaches

Other possible responses include:

- register: informal and lighthearted
- coherence: FAQ style, conventions of an email, inference

Mark allocation: 4 marks

- 1 mark for accurately identifying a way that social distance is reduced and rapport is built
- 3 marks for analysis of how two examples support your claim about social distance and rapport using appropriate metalanguage

TIP

» **It is a good idea to select an area of focus and develop it. If your answer to the 'how' is 'register', give examples of register. This will create a cogent response; otherwise, you risk a list of various and unconnected examples.**

Question 3

Sample response

Both the heading 'Screenshotting is out' (16) and the compound sentence that opens the subsequent section, 'It's ... tickets' (17), are intended to summarise the relevant information about avoiding screenshotting tickets. A rhetorical interrogative 'Why?' (18) invites readers to consider the justification, if they do not take the advice at face value. This leads onto a compound-complex sentence, 'Because ... their ticket' (18–21), which uses humour to maintain interest. The multiple clauses give the impression of frustration that is experienced by those 'stuck' (18,19) in the queue described.

The imperative verbs in line 22, 'Be smarter than that and use the app instead', serve a conative function, and the independent clauses can stand alone so that the length and complexity of the subsequent clause 'because...' (22–23) is additional information that may be skipped or read as needed.

Other approaches

Other possible aspects of syntax include:

- phrases: 'at the entry gate behind the person' (18–19)
- active voice: 'use the app instead' (22)
- patterning – listing: line 23
- adverbials: 'Because your time is Priceless' (18)

Mark allocation: 3 marks

- 1 mark for accurately identifying a syntactic feature in the highlighted lines
- 2 marks for discussing the function of the identified syntactic feature with appropriate metalanguage

TIP

» **The sample response is longer than necessary and the first paragraph alone would garner 3 marks.**

Question 4

Sample response

> Ticketmaster uses semantic patterning as the titles of Light's songs are puns in the email. The adjectives 'Priceless' (18) and 'Delightful' (24), and the noun phrase 'The Path' (39) are all used relevantly in their sentences but the capitalisation of each makes them proper nouns that are puns for Light's song titles. 'Hector's House' (8) is used similarly, however here there is semantic ambiguity as the House could refer to the show or Light's home, as well as the album title. The readership of fans will likely find this fun, increasing rapport, which may prompt them to follow the instructions given about ticketing. Finally, 'thirst traps' (31) is a metaphor for attractive photographs and plays on the original idiom 'honey trap'. This metaphor is commonly used in social media and has appeal for the target audience, who engage with the singer through these mediums and will be familiar with the behaviour described, creating humour and reducing the social distance.
>
> Morphological patterning is used in the shortening of 'congratulations' to 'Congrats!' (3) to mimic the spoken mode and reduce the social distance between the reader and the company. Likewise, 'fandoms' (50) is a compounding that acknowledges Light's fans as a unique social group whose identity is linked to the singer, evidenced in the adjoining adjective: 'dedicated fandoms'.

Other approaches

Other possible examples include:

- 'Screenshotting is out' (16), with morphological patterning in the conversion of 'screenshotting'.

Mark allocation: 5 marks

- The 5 marks are awarded holistically. The discussion should include at least three patterns across the two subsystems. You'll receive marks in the low/low–medium range if you identify patterns but do not develop the discussion or do not consider both subsystems. To score highly, you need to select relevant patterns in both subsystems and consider their use in relation to the specifics of text – the situational context, the audience, the purpose, social groups and so forth.
  - 4 to 5 marks: Demonstrates detailed knowledge and is supported by relevant examples/evidence from the text. Metalanguage is used appropriately and effectively. Features of written discourse are consistently used.
  - 2 to 3 marks: Demonstrates sound knowledge and is supported by some examples/evidence from the text. The metalanguage used is relevant. Some features of written discourse are evident.
  - 0 to 1 mark: Demonstrates limited knowledge and contains few examples from the text. The use of metalanguage is limited or absent. Few features of written discourse are evident.

TIPS

- **Ensure you discuss both subsystems, as the question stipulates.**
- **Ensure you label the pattern in each instance – the specific word formation process or affixation; the particular type of figurative language.**

TEXT G

Question 1

Sample response

The alliteration of the [d] consonant in 'dare to dream of a Docklands that isn't dreadful' (1–2) is intended to capture the reader's attention in the headline and indicate the two possible outcomes for the area: 'dream' or 'dreadful', which are connected through the alliteration.

Other approaches

- In 'perplexing planning and political legacy' (6) the [p] alliteration and [l] consonance makes it complex to read and this reflects the complexity of the idea being expressed
- 'varied and vitriolic' (8), alliteration of [v] consonant
- 'Docklands ... colossal policy ... produced ... avoidable eyesore' (9–10), assonance of [ɔ] phoneme

Mark allocation: 2 marks

- 1 mark for accurately identifying a phonological pattern, with a quote and metalanguage
- 1 mark for explaining the effect of this example

Question 2

Sample response

Sense relations are used to encourage the audience to want to improve the suburb of the Docklands. *The Age* uses connotations of abandonment in the noun phrase 'maze of asphalt' (59), the adjective 'empty' (59) and the compound noun 'dead-ends' (59) to create a negative picture of the area, encouraging the idea that it needs attention to improve it. The alternative possibilities for the suburb are also built through antonymy in the noun phrases 'concrete jungle' and 'vibrant hub' on line 13 and the nouns 'wasteland' and 'oasis' in line 23. The positively connotated options of 'hub' and 'oasis' inspire the reader to choose this option in each antonym.

Other approaches

- idioms: 'rust bucket' (21), 'city of dreams' (21)
- connotations of carelessness in the noun phrase 'free-market thinking' (31) and the borrowing 'laissez-faire' (32)
- hypernym 'amenities' (44) with hyponyms 'parks' (44), 'schools' (45), 'cultural sites' (45), 'apartment towers' (46), 'offices' (47), 'library' (51).

Mark allocation: 4 marks

- This question should be marked holistically, using the guide below.
  - 4 marks: The response demonstrates a detailed knowledge of the text and is supported by relevant examples/evidence. Metalanguage is used appropriately and effectively. Features of written discourse are consistently used.
  - 2 to 3 marks: The response demonstrates a sound knowledge of the text and is supported by some examples/evidence. The metalanguage used is relevant. Some features of written discourse are evident.
  - 0 to 1 mark: The response demonstrates a limited knowledge of the text and contains few examples. The use of metalanguage is limited or absent. Few features of written discourse are evident.

TIPS

- **The question asks for two different examples. This means you should select two different types of sense relations, rather than two different examples of the same sense relation.**
- **Sense relations are synonymy, antonymy, hyponymy, hypernymy, idiom, denotation and connotation.**
- **Although the question asks for two different examples, because it is marked holistically it is a good idea to link your examples together in an overarching argument. This will also help create a coherent 'discussion', as the question requires.**

Question 3

Sample response

The tenor is socially distant but *The Age* also creates a sense of colluding with the reader, so although the register is formal, there are examples of face threatening language that generate slight informality. For example, the Docklands is described in a noun phrase as a 'colossal policy failure' (9), which threatens the negative face both of politicians who created the policy and Melbournians who are proud of their city. This is mitigated by the informal adjective 'smidgen' (11), which positions the government as being able to fix the issue easily and appeases the Melbournians who are invited to collude in shifting the responsibility onto the government.

Other approaches: *The Age* creates an in-group of Melbournians and Docklands residents and sets them against the government and politicians, so the formal register is dominated with harsh phrases and rhetoric criticising the government such as 'But reality bit' (29), 'the fast-pace parcelling up and selling of chunks of land' (41) and 'defined by its flaws' (56).

Mark allocation: 4 marks

- This question should be marked holistically, using the guide below.
  - 4 marks: The response demonstrates a detailed knowledge of the text and is supported by relevant examples/evidence. Metalanguage is used appropriately and effectively. Features of written discourse are consistently used.
  - 2 to 3 marks: The response demonstrates a sound knowledge of the text and is supported by some examples/evidence. The metalanguage used is relevant. Some features of written discourse are evident.
  - 0 to 1 mark: The response demonstrates a limited knowledge of the text and contains few examples. The use of metalanguage is limited or absent. Few features of written discourse are evident.

TIP

» **This is a hard text and a hard question! Practising on difficult texts and questions improves your confidence for exams.**

Question 4

Sample response

The Age intends to influence the government to take action to improve the Docklands. To achieve this, they use complex sentence structures and declarative sentence types. The complex declarative sentence in lines 61–62 begins with an adverbial 'At *The Age*,' to identify themselves as giving advice. The start of the subsequent independent clause and embedded dependent clause, 'we believe that it is time ... precinct' (61), outlines the importance of immediate action, with a final dependent clause 'that it can be improved' (62) to indicate what action they want. The subsequent complex sentence begins with a dependent clause to indicate what the government should *not* do – 'While it may be tempting ...' (62–63) – before using end focus in the independent clause to say what the government *should* do – 'they would be wiser ...' (63–64). This use of declarative sentences achieves their persuasive intent of motivating the government to take action on the 'opportunity' (64) offered by the Docklands.

Other approaches

- In lines 13–26, you could refer to listing in lines 15–17; a short simple sentence as contrast in line 22; embedded clauses in lines 19–20; parallelism in 22–23; modifiers in the noun phrases in 15–17.
- Other elements of syntax include complements, adverbials, ellipsis, and active and passive voice.

Mark allocation: 5 marks

- This question should be marked holistically, using the guide below.
  - 4 to 5 marks: The response demonstrates a detailed knowledge of the text and is supported by relevant examples/evidence. Metalanguage is used appropriately and effectively. Features of written discourse are consistently used.
  - 2 to 3 marks: The response demonstrates a sound knowledge of the text and is supported by some examples/evidence. The metalanguage used is relevant. Some features of written discourse are evident.
  - 0 to 1 mark: The response demonstrates a limited knowledge of the text and contains few examples. The use of metalanguage is limited or absent. Few features of written discourse are evident.

Section B: Analytical commentary

Mark allocation: 30 marks

- Section B is marked holistically based on the criteria provided by VCAA. To score in the higher bands, the analysis should be wide-ranging, providing examples from throughout the text, rather than focusing on only one or two particular sections. A higher-scoring response must acknowledge the shifts in register and tie this to the purpose(s).

TIPS

» Be selective in what you analyse in Section B; it is important to prioritise the characteristics and subsystem features that are most relevant to the text type, as it is impossible to address everything.

» Select and discuss the language features that are most closely connected to the text's register, context and purpose(s). Features should not be discussed in isolation.

» Give at least one example from the text for every feature discussed and remember to cite line numbers.

» Avoid generalities such as giving a definition of the feature or saying what the feature usually does rather than what it is doing in this particular example.

» When analysing spoken texts, always refer to speakers by name and link features you are analysing back to the speaker.

» Remember to explore several aspects of situational context: mode, text type, tenor, setting and field. Where relevant to the text, you should also look to engage in a discussion of cultural context and/or the identity or identities constructed in the text.

» While there is no specific structure for Section B, if you arrange your response according to subsystem, you may limit your opportunities for discussion. Your response should be well organised and in paragraphs. Subheadings may be appropriate to help organise some responses and you will not be penalised if you use them effectively.

» Your first paragraph should include an identification of the text and author/interlocutors. This can be an introduction that also mentions purpose(s), register (including the degree of formality), tenor and any relevant elements of situational and/or cultural context that you will be discussing. Alternatively, these can be introduced as they become relevant in your discussion, and you can leave out an introduction beyond identification of the text in the first paragraph. Be aware that without examples and metalanguage, an introduction can only contribute to your grade by improving the structural elements of your commentary, so keep it short if you use it.

» No conclusion paragraph is required, but you should nevertheless aim to give the piece a sense of completion.

» Be aware of a range of possible organisational strategies before sitting the exam so that you can be flexible in your approach and respond in the most effective way to the text in front of you.

TEXT H

Sample response

The text is a promotional video from Business Victoria in the spoken mode that includes written and visual elements from the video. Its purpose is to promote the business Clothing The Gap and share advice for other small business owners. To this end, the two co-founders in the video, Laura Thompson and Sarah Sheridan, adopt a moderately informal register that maintains a supportive and personable tenor throughout.

Thompson and Sheridan build the identity of the organisation as one that is socially conscious and reflective of the community it represents. This is captured in the video's scripted opening, in which Thompson uses parallelism to link 'community' (1) with 'fashion' (2) through the repetition of the verb 'changing' (1 and 2), giving viewers an immediate impression of the company's values and merchandise. The rhetorical interrogative in line 5, 'why wouldn't you choose those brands?', subtly promotes their t-shirts and hat through the inference that the determiner 'those' also refers to brands in the visual on line 6. This way, they address a promotional purpose while also giving advice to other small businesses that they should try to have a 'social impact' (3–4). Thompson further builds the company's social credentials and community focus by associating emotion with the brand through the verbs 'love' (33) and 'celebrating' (37) and the verb phrase 'makes us feel good' (36). Sheridan creates a personable impression though the hypocoristic use of 'cuppa' (42), which she is willing to share with 'anyone' (41) in the community. In combination, this gives the brand a sense of warmth and approachability that is designed to build rapport with potential customers and model good business practices to those looking for advice.

Thompson also builds her own identity, introducing herself as a 'Gunditjmara woman' (7) which defines her cultural identity as an Aboriginal Australian. This is further supported by her at times Broad Australian accent, seen in 'try'n tell' (16) and 'youda' (17) which elides the function words 'and' and 'to' to assimilate them with their preceding content words. She also uses uptalk (12, 16, 20) to hold the floor and maintain the attention of her listeners (evidenced by Sheridan's minimal response 'yeah' in line 13), which is a common feature of Australian intonation. This personal identity establishes her as an authority in a business that is both for and by Aboriginal Australians. When she draws on the noun phrase 'my cultural heritage' (57), she is established as an expert, and this validates her subsequent opinion that the company's clothes are 'art' (59), which has positive connotations, and that the clothes 'express ... identity 'n culcha' (60), which she is now in a valid position to judge.

Sheridan's role in the discourse is to manage the topics, though she most often cedes the floor to Thompson, as seen in lines 10–11 when she states the business's main product before allowing Thompson to retake the floor after the overlapping speech '[start up]' and '[yeah]' (12–13). The topic of selecting a name for the brand is managed by Thompson, who recounts the process alongside an image of a social media post with '122 likes' (19) that demonstrates community engagement. The business name is a pun on 'closing the gap', a collocation that is well known in the Australian cultural context and which refers to reducing inequalities between Indigenous Australians and other Australians, including in terms of life expectancy. Thompson uses the positively connotated verbs 'resonated' (20) and 'engage' (23) to describe the response to the name 'Clothing The Gap'. This is also supported by the image of the social media post with heart emojis (22), which offers supplementary pragmatic information that indicates a warmly emotive tenor. In her next turn, Sheridan becomes the voice of non-Indigenous Australia, positioning herself using the generalised noun 'everybody' (25) to invite non-Indigenous Australians to feel comfortable that they are also welcome to enjoy the brand, thus addressing their negative face needs in what can be a culturally sensitive topic.

The text's overt purpose is to give advice to small business owners but is has a secondary purpose of promoting the brand. Sheridan lowers her register a little, using humour to imply that having a business is a lot of work. She does this when she shifts topic in her exclamative sentence 'There's so much to lea=rn!' (43); the elongation of the vowel sound draws attention to how challenging this is. This segues into a list of roles the two co-founders have in the company (46–48), using the third item in Sheridan's list to raise the last topic, 'planning for the future' (48). This gives other potential small business owners a sense of the scope of what is needed to run a successful business for a long time – both practical aspects, seen in the nouns from the field of business such as 'HR' (46) and 'accounting' (47), but also having a vision and strong values. Sheridan and Thompson imply that their success is built from their focus on social media and their support of the Aboriginal community. Other businesses are encouraged to make the most of social media through the emphatic adverb in the verb phrase 'we absolutely love' (53) and the noun phrase 'genuine tool' (55), which has connotations of usefulness and value. Sheridan uses metaphors to describe their support of the Aboriginal community, explaining she 'cheer[s] on' (66) others who are 'kicking massive goals' (68). This supportive register uses metaphors drawn from the field of football to build a sense of community support and in-group other Aboriginal businesses. Thompson's closing returns to the pun in the brand name in the final declarative that has both an emotive and poetic function, to 'make sure that we're around here to keep adding years to people's lives' (76–77). The implication is that viewers should support the company because it is emotionally and politically virtuous. This is furthered by the visual, which uses the informal collocation 'get behind' (79) in conjunction with the company's website to fulfil the promotional purpose.

TEXT I

Sample response

The text is a bulletin in written mode that was posted online at a Victorian high school. It was written by the school's Student Services and provides students with advice on preparing themselves to return to school after the summer holidays. Given the text has a referential function, there are features of formal language to establish expertise. However, informal language has also been employed to create a sense of familiarity and build a rapport between the Student Services Team and students.

The text's purpose is to build trust and offer supportive advice to the students reading it. This is reinforced through the use of informal language. Though the text is written, Students Services frequently imitate the spoken mode to create a more personable register and a warm tenor that is reflective of a close social distance like that of a trusted friend or mentor. For example, the interjection 'Ah, summer' on line 2 as an opening to the article creates a sense of nostalgia that is supposedly shared by both the students and Student Services, which counters the impression the students might have that the Services do not understand their negative feelings about their return to school. In addition, 'Well' (14) and 'So' (41) function as discourse particles, as they would in the spoken mode, to casually introduce the next point about how to cope when returning to school after the holidays have ended. The repeated use of the second-person pronoun 'you' (2, 19, 35, 55) helps reduce the social distance between the author and intended audience, making the students feel they are being spoken to directly. For example, the pronoun's use in line 7 introduces a list of possible student concerns with the verb phrase 'maybe you're thinking', in which the direct address implies students are well understood by Student Services, who know their inner minds. The pronoun and positively connotated verb 'We hope' on line 57 personalises Student Services' interest in students, while the pronoun use in 'we all' (42) and 'us all' (59) evokes a feeling of commonality through the generalisation, functioning as inclusive pronouns. Lexis that is more colloquial – such as the metaphor 'hanging out' (2) and the hypocoristic suffix in 'footy' (34) – further supports the informal and personable register of the text. These are terms that might be used among young friends, therefore making the text more relatable to the intended audience. The final exclamative on line 61, 'You got this!', is non-Standard due to the ellipsis of the auxiliary verb 'have', thus ensuring the article closes with a sense of support and optimism.

As the text also advises students on how to prepare themselves for a return to school, and has a focus on health and wellbeing, formal and clarifying language has been employed. This aids Student Services in establishing their expertise and authority in this area, which is also important as other school staff and the parent/carer community have access to the online article. To this end, professional lexemes, such as the verb 'engages' (20) and the nominalisation 'judgement' (24), are used. In addition, the listing of strategies from the RAIN formula (22–29) indicates a level of authority. The way the information is laid out also adds to the text's authority. The information is ordered logically, beginning with the declarative that 'the holidays can't last forever' (4) which serves an emotive function, expressing regret at the end of the holiday, before shifting to more referential declaratives with 'suggestions that might help' (15) with the return to school and routines. The text is closed with the phatic acknowledgement that they will soon 'enter 2023' (59) and that students 'just need to take it one day at a time' (60–61), which is conative as it supports their feelings while also acting as advice. Similarly, the bolded title of the article on line 1, 'Tackling the Back-to-School Blues', and the three bolded subheadings, the first being 'Talk about your feelings' (16), all direct the reader to what information will follow. This logical ordering not only allows Student Services to clarify each point, it also establishes a coherent text that invites the young readers to engage with the information and tips, fulfilling its main advisory purpose.

The intent of the authors is to reach out to the student population of this school to ensure they feel positive and ready for a new school year, and depict themselves as approachable should students need support. Therefore, lexis from the field of wellbeing has been used throughout the text, including the adverb 'mindfully' (18), noun 'feelings' (19), verb phrase 'feel better' (29), adjective 'relaxation' (38) and verb 'support' (58). In contemporary society, looking after mental health has become part of the culture of schools. This text exemplifies that this school values the wellbeing of their students. Student Services acts on the school's behalf to create a persona of a caring community that also values learning. Hence, nouns and noun phrases such as 'school timetable' (31), 'homework' (36) and 'school' (58) are used to highlight that the article has been sourced from the school, while the verbs indicate care and advice, as in 'create' (46), the phrasal verb 'lay off' (49) and the collocation 'keep calm' (51).

TIP

» **You can engage with the text by referring to the author(s) and intended audience specifically. In this case, the author is Student Services and the intended audience is the student body.**

TEXT J

Sample response

Text J is a speech delivered by Senator Penny Wong at Youth Voice in Parliament Week which she draws in part from Winter Birkett, a young woman in her electorate. The register is formal and heartfelt and Wong's purposes include encouraging equality for women in government, reinforcing her authority and establishing her expertise as a senator in the Australian Parliament.

The topic of gender equality in the Australian Parliament is reinforced through the lexical repetition of 'girls' (14, 18, 22, 24, 27) and 'women' (8, 12, 24, 37, 38, 42). This factor of cohesion reinforces the point that it is girls and women for whom the push for equality is needed. Wong's formal register is evidenced in her use of the proper noun phrase 'Youth Voice in Parliament Week' (4) to establish the importance of the occasion and includes an honorific when she mentions 'Ms Winter Birkett' (5), a mark of respect to the young woman whose words she is relaying to the senators in front of her. As it is a formal setting, there is a high level of planning, seen through the front focus of adverbials 'As such' (14), 'However' (25) and 'Currently' (26), which contribute to the cohesion of the speech by providing a logical order as Wong moves from one point to the next. Planning is also apparent through careful placing of adverbs in front of verbs, such as 'actively discouraged' (18–19) and 'politically interested' (26–27). Nominalisation and a sophisticated lexis also contribute to the formal register in 'representation' (12) and 'permeates' (29). The Latinate phrase 'status quo' (25) further supports the formal register and all of this gives the speech a sense of gravitas.

Through her speech, Wong intends to promote gender equality for girls and women. To build her authority in this, she opens her speech with a sentence including the prepositional phrase 'on behalf of' (1). By positioning herself as a mouthpiece for her constituent she builds her identity as a listener and as a politician that cares about her electorate and by extension the voice of the Australian public. Wong lists Birkett's credentials, relevant in the setting of the Youth Voice event, with synonymy that emphasises Birkett's youth, using the adjective 'young' (2), the noun phrase 'as part of Youth ... Week' (4) and her age: '17 years old' (5). This justifies Wong's authority on the issue – she is drawing on a youthful voice – and conversely, gives that voice authority when it is delivered by an elected senator.

Birkett's message is to empower women and girls to '<u>aspire</u> to one day become politicians' (16). The verb '<u>aspire</u>' has connotations of hope, as does the adverb 'one day' and Wong's stress on the verb has a conative function, inviting listeners to hold the aspiration for themselves. Wong's use of pauses in 'is (.) not (.) good enough\' (9) adds weight to the statistic that shows women are under-represented in Australian politics. The falling pitch to end this utterance adds further to the gravity. In combination, the audience is invited to be part of a solution to bring about the hoped-for future of equal representation. In addition, stress gives prominence to important terms such as the determiner '<u>all</u>' (29) and adverb '<u>now</u>' (31), and on syllables in adjectives such as '<u>up</u>lifted' and 'empowered' (22). Stress underlines both the immediacy of the need and the positive outcomes available if the call to action is heeded by the audience. Stress is also applied to the modal verbs 'can' (11) and 'must' (13, 25, 31), indicating that the voting audience have the capability and obligation to encourage gender equality in society, particularly in politics.

Wong uses an intake of breath on line 35 to manage the topic shift back to her own words. In this section of her speech, Wong establishes her expertise and authority from her position in Australian politics. She provides referential declaratives such as 'Labor now has more women than men in the Senate' (38), indicating that she knows the facts of the issue. She refers to the positively connotated 'affirmative action targets' (39) that have led to this success and invites the audience to infer that Labor is alone in this, since she calls upon other parties, using the determiner 'all' (41) to 'mandate targets' (42). This also uses lexical repetition in 'targets' to emphasise the action she wants taken in relation to the issues she raises, reiterating her role and authority as a senator.

Birkett and Wong's words reflect Australian values of inclusiveness and gender equality. There is repetition in Birkett's speech, delivered by Wong, when she says 'in 20 years' (14, 23), providing a vision of what she wants to see in the world. Terms such as 'representation' (12) and 'diverse' (15) are words we associate with contemporary Australian society, a society which strives for equity across all spheres. As a female senator, Wong shows that she agrees with Birkett, and she ends the speech by calling for 'equal women's representation' (42). This is spoken at a slow pace, which emphasises the importance of the matter.

TIP

- **There might be features one student includes in their analytical commentary that another does not. As long as the features are salient, this is acceptable. For example, there are stylistic features such as figurative language (21, 29–30) that have not been included in this commentary but would be completely acceptable features to include.**

TEXT K

Sample response

This formal written text about the feral horses in Victoria's Alpine National Park was published on the Parks Victoria website in May 2020. It is a press release to inform an audience of environmentalists, farmers, animal rights advocates, and those who visit the region, of the outcome of the Federal Court decision to cull the invasive species. As well as clarifying details of the issue for the public, it also promotes Parks Victoria as a government organisation that understands the importance of the region's flora and fauna.

The purpose of the press release is to update interested parties on the outcome of a legal case involving Parks Victoria and the Australian Brumby Alliance (ABA). The formatting assists to clarify the stance of Parks Victoria with the bolded headline that begins with a positively connotated verb, 'Protecting the Alpine National Park' (1). The outcome of the case is stated below in a subheading, 'Federal Court finds in favour of Parks Victoria' (3) which uses simple present tense to build an objective register. In addition to this, Parks Victoria uses referential declarative sentences, such as 'The Federal Court of Australia has today delivered its judgement ...' (4) and 'The ABA had sought an injunction to stop Parks Victoria ...' (9), in the body of the text to clarify a timeline of actions taken. The repetition of 'Parks Victoria' throughout the text (lines 3, 5, 6, 9, 12, 16, 23, 36) highlights their role in the legal case and their plans for the animals; however, the verb phrases obfuscate the fact that the outcome means horses will be killed, evidenced in the euphemistic and nominalised 'undertaking removal' (9) and 'obligation to reduce' (16). Instead, adjectives have been selected to present Parks Victoria as an organisation that has environmental protection as a key priority. The horses are described using the adjective 'feral' (7), which has connotations of being problematic and intrusive. This is further supported by their impact being described with the adjective 'severe' (7) and the noun 'damage' (27). In contrast, the Alpine National Park garners the adjective 'iconic' (7) and the wildlife, plants and habitats are labelled using the adjective 'fragile' (27). These lexical choices position the reader to side with the decision of the Federal Court, building support for Parks Victoria's push to preserve the natural environment by using 'control' (37), which is another euphemism for killing the brumbies and obfuscates a potentially unpopular decision. The release further promotes Parks Victoria as an organisation that is proactive by using modal verbs in 'will be commencing' (36) and 'will be deployed' (37) to show certainty that Parks Victoria is going to follow through with their proposed actions.

The press release has a formal and objective register. It is logically ordered and formatted into paragraphs, starting with the 'Federal Court ... judgement' (4) before explaining what occurred 'Over the past 18 months' (23) and finally the 'longer-term program' (43). Adverbials such as 'During this period' (29) also show planning, and they are set off by a comma before the main clause. As required in a formal written text, proper nouns are always capitalised, such as 'Alpine National Park' (8) and '*Environment Protection and Biodiversity Conservation Act 1999*' (14–15). The initialism 'ABA' has been used on line 5 in order to avoid redundantly repeating the entire noun phrase 'Australian Brumby Alliance' on line 9, but it also adheres to a convention adopted by bureaucratic and government texts, as word formations such as initialisms and acronyms are commonly used. Bureaucratic lexis similarly supports the formal register and indicates the professionalism of Parks Victoria's media team, including 'Stephanie Zilles' (49). Modifiers such as the adverb 'subsequently' (26) and adjective 'comprehensive' (29) indicate the strategic approach taken by Parks Victoria, with the denotation of 'comprehensive' highlighting their expertise and professionalism due to the extensive considerations made. Additionally, 'equine' (40) uses scientific jargon to add specificity to the discussion. 'Commencing' on line 36 is also a more formal verb choice than 'starting'. As well as this, lexis from the field of law, such as 'judgement' (4) and 'injunction' (9), supports the formal and objective register, and is appropriate given the context of this text, which is providing clarity around a legal issue. The use of the passive voice is a typical feature of formal language, and it has been used on lines 24–25 with 'Trapping and rehoming programs that <u>were previously implemented</u> ...' and 'Small-team operations <u>will be deployed</u> ...' (37). These passives function to remove the agent, Parks Victoria, shifting the focus to the actions that were or will be carried out and reducing the responsibility of the organisation if the audience members such as animal rights advocates disagree with the action taken on the horses.

In the Australian cultural context, the preservation of the country's unique environment is valued by most of its inhabitants, and this report appeals to that by using lexical items from the domain of the environment such as 'native wildlife' and 'ecosystems' (34). 'National Heritage' is given proper noun status when mentioning the impact on 'values' (22). Despite this, most people would decry animal cruelty, so the text reinforces the humane treatment of the horses with lists of mitigating adjectives in the noun phrases 'professional shooters' (38–39), 'strict animal welfare protocols' (40) and 'expert equine veterinary oversight' (40–41), to reassure those concerned.

TIP

» **Dull texts are hardest to write about, so you need to be particularly careful to avoid generic analysis. Often students fall back on defining the features or listing examples without offering much insight into the text. To avoid this, always consider the purpose and intent. Ask yourself who is trying to achieve what? What does the writer or speaker stand to lose or gain? In this text, the dense and dispassionate writing obscures the fact that the government is planning to kill horses! So that is your way in – if you look at their language choices from that angle, it becomes much more interesting.**

TEXT L

Sample response

The foreword to Nakkiah Lui's play *Black is the New White* is written in a register that has both formal and informal language features. It provides the reader with Lui's rationale for writing her play and, as a result, Lui builds rapport with her readership as they get to know more about her, her family and her experiences as an Aboriginal woman in Australia. The mostly declarative sentences provide the audience with some context about the play they are about to read, with the interrogatives giving the reader a sense of the play's origins. These features help Lui to achieve the purpose of engaging the reader in the play.

Lui achieves coherence through lexical repetition of the adjective 'Aboriginal' (e.g. 15, 20, 22), as Lui's identity and experiences as an Aboriginal person are the focus of her play. Semantically, cohesion is achieved through the use of lexical items from the domain of family, with the nouns 'family' (1, 35, 44), 'cousin' (14) and 'parents' (22) featuring throughout the text, often with positively connoted adjectival phrases accompanying them, such as 'fabulous' (15) for her cousin, and 'culturally quite strong' (43) for her family. These terms, while having a semantic link, also show the reader that family is important to Lui. There is also Lui's application of lexis from the semantic field of the arts, such as 'play' (12) and 'canon' (42), which forms part of her identity as a person working in the entertainment industry. Another aspect of her identity is her Aboriginality, and this is repeatedly referred to on lines 22 and 25 when she refers to her parents and being 'Aboriginal middle class'. Lui meets the face needs of her Aboriginal community by employing capital letters for the adjectives 'Black' and 'Blacker' (19). This use of capitalisation elevates these terms to show they are important to Lui and her community and models this respect for the reader. Inference is required on lines 40 to 43 when Lui states that she wishes to present an Aboriginal family 'that hasn't been seen before' (41), a family with money who 'are not necessarily oppressed' (43). Here it is inferred that much of the literature to date depicts Aboriginal families as poor (inferred from the adverbial 'who have money', 42) or oppressed (inferred from the adjective phrase 'not necessarily oppressed', 43), motivating her to shift the group's perceived identity through her work.

As this text is distributed by publishers Allen & Unwin, and Lui is a professional writer and playwright, the foreword adheres to the expectations of language that appears in publications of this nature. Features of Standard English are employed: initial lexemes in sentences are capitalised (such as 'A family that is changing ... a loved one leaving', 10–11) and mostly standard punctuation is used, with commas separating clauses (e.g. 9, 38). Proper nouns such as 'Christmas' (1) and the title of her play, *Black is the New White* (13), have also been capitalised. These features of Standard English ensure the information is clearly communicated to the reader, and the text is coherent. Lui's identity as a respected writer also influences the register, with some parts made more formal through use of lexical and syntactic features. For example, Lui contrasts sophisticated lexis such as the noun 'sacrilege' (2), adverb 'vastly' (34) and verb 'politicised' (40) with the hashtag given to the compound noun '#yummymummy' used on line 16. She also deliberately constructs sentences with adverbials such as 'Primarily' (30) as the initial lexeme, and a range of sentence structures are used, which shows deliberate planning. For example, in the first paragraph, the simple opening sentence on line 1, 'I love Christmas', is followed by a complex sentence on lines 8–9, 'I love watching Christmas movies ...', which contains dependent clauses set off by the subordinating conjunctions 'that' (8) and 'whilst' (9).

However, Lui does lower the register in order to achieve one of her purposes, which is to build rapport with her audience. Her tone can be quite conversational, as evidenced by her use of syntactic patterning in the consecutive simple sentences 'I love Christmas. My family love Christmas' (1). Some of her sentences also start with coordinating conjunctions, such as 'But' on lines 12 and 33, and 'So' on line 43. This is in contrast to the adverb 'However' on line 22, which would be considered more formal. Punctuation and contractions are also used to help Lui imitate the spoken mode, suggesting a closer tenor. Parentheses allow her to provide a personal aside on line 17 '(talking politics ... my family)', and ellipses on lines 19 and 28 function to represent pauses. Contractions 'didn't' (20) and 'I'd' (31) also reinforce this more casual register. The repeated use of the personal pronoun 'I' throughout the text helps Lui fulfil her aim to reduce the social distance between author and reader. She does this by repeating the pronoun while affording readers an insight into her interests ('I love watching Christmas movies', 8); her sense of humour about her experiences ('I had dated one Aboriginal person ... they turned out to be a cousin', 20–21); and her political identity ('I was really interested in how we identity ourselves', 36–37). The interrogatives interspersed among the declarative sentences – such as 'However, ... why didn't I?' (22–23) and 'What does it mean to be successful?' (38–39) – provide insight into Lui's identity as a person who questions herself and her world. Lui also shares a conversation with her cousin who says that sticking together will ensure the community becomes 'bigger and better and Blacker' (18–19), which Lui indicates with speech marks and uses to present her family as holding varied views, using alliteration to promote this as positive.

As a writer and playwright, Lui establishes her expertise and fulfils the purpose of engaging her audience. Lui's use of descriptive language in the declarative on line 9 ('sweat it out in front of a fan'), for example, serves a poetic function and assumes the Australian audience has experienced the country's hot summers and will relate to the image presented. Lui employs alliterative adjectives to describe her 'gorgeous' and 'great' (15) cousin, and lists that she is 'a lover of Instagram and lycra and the hashtag #yummymummy' (15–16). To produce a sense of rhythm, Lui also uses syntactic features such as parallelism, repeating the subject–verb construction 'I love', 'My family love' (1) to start a number of her sentences in the opening paragraph. These are deliberate language features that serve a poetic function and in doing so engage the audience and provide insight into the playwright's identity and expertise.

TIP

» **When analysing a written text, features of coherence and cohesion are particularly important to include in your discussion.**

TEXT M

Sample response

The extract from the television show *Q+A* demonstrates a semi-prepared interaction between host Tony Jones and guest panellist Eddie Woo. Woo responds to a prepared question from Miriam Lees, an audience member, with the aim to present Woo's point of view on why people find it easy to admit to being poor mathematicians and to provide insight into what he believes makes a good teacher. The broad purpose of the conversational exchange is to entertain an Australian audience, those present as well as those watching at home, with an intellectual discussion on the features that create good teachers. This particular portion of the show focuses on mathematics, and, as such, lexical choices from the field of mathematics appear: for example, Jones' jargonistic use of the nouns 'hypotenuse' (64), 'sum' (65) and 'squares' (65).

In his role as host, Tony Jones delivers a prepared, formal opening. While very short pauses are used throughout the opening (1, 4, 5 etc.), these pauses are carefully placed to segue between descriptions of panellists rather than demonstrating evidence of non-fluency. This is seen in the declarative 'teacher turned <u>champion</u> ... (.) Pasi <u>Sahlberg</u>' (3–4) and 'Indigenous teacher and advocate (.) Cindy <u>Berwick</u>' (10). The somewhat cataphoric nature of these descriptions provides an element of suspense to Jones' introduction. The descriptions also meet the face needs of his guests, as the formal adjectives and nouns he uses to describe them tend towards flattery: such as with 'award-winning' (9) as an adjective to describe Eddie Woo, 'champion' (4) as a noun to label Pasi Sahlberg and 'stellar' (17) as an adjective to describe all of the panellists. Reinforcing his role as host, Jones formally invites the participating audience of 'students/ parents/ (.) and teachers\' (18) to 'welcome our panel' (11), with the imperative modified by the adverb 'please' to soften the command. Jones uses a formal register in the opening as this is required as part of his duties as host. Further, by elevating the status of his guests when introducing them and using politeness markers with his audience, Jones appears knowledgeable, competent and respectful.

As part of the context of *Q+A*, audience members are invited to ask questions of panellists. In the text, audience member Miriam Lees is invited to ask her question by Jones' use of the declarative 'and our first question/ (.) comes from Miriam <u>Lees</u>' (19). Lees demonstrates nervousness when asking her pre-prepared question, as the beginning of her turn contains a number of non-fluency features. False starts such as 'go- good evening' (20) and fillers such as 'um' (21) are evidence of this. While Lees participates in the topic-initiation sequence of asking why people are so willing to admit to being poor mathematicians, she does not take any further turns in the conversational exchange; in this context, her participation is complete as soon as the interrogative 'Why do you think that's the case?' (25) is asked.

Jones reinforces his role as host by directing Woo to respond to Lees' question. After his formal introduction of Woo, he reduces social distance by using vocative first name 'Eddie' (26) to direct Woo to respond. He also uses the adverb 'obviously' in end focus in line 26 to imply that there is good reason for Woo to provide the first response. Woo uses cohesive front focus to inform the audience of this reason – he is 'a mathematics teacher' (27) – and emphasise his relevant expertise. This technique reinforces coherence and is inclusive of Woo; it demonstrates Jones' ability to successfully maintain the positive face needs of the audience so that they are not excluded. Woo's use of declarative anecdotes when providing his point of view acts to render the register more casual, and also presents a humble and personable identity to the *Q+A* audience. His selection of the verb 'struggled' (30) helps to achieve this as it carries connotations of long-term difficulties in relation to his time learning mathematics at school. This humility is marked enough for Jones to interrupt Woo, with a non-fluent overlap occurring mid-utterance in lines 31 and 32. Jones does this to manage the topic; he asks a clarifying question so Woo will elaborate: 'so wait you weren't a maths genius when you were at school?' (32), which contains the colloquial discourse particle 'so'. This reinforces Jones' role as host while also reducing the register and allowing Woo to demonstrate aspects of a humble identity, with the appearance of the vocal effect of laughter in his self-deprecating admission that he is '@@still @not a maths @ genius now' (33). The reduced formality from both speakers as the segment progresses allows the exchange to appear more conversational and appeal to an Australian audience, who appreciate humility in the face of success.

Woo's participation in the exchange contains frequent non-fluency features, demonstrating that his responses are not carefully prepared. While he may have an idea as to what he will say, he has not prepared a word-for-word response to the question he was asked. This can be seen with fillers ('uh', 34, 38), false starts ('s- sense', 29; 'it is-- you know', 43; 'w- we're', 55), and pauses mid-utterance such as those seen in lines 36 ('a sense of (.) wanting') and 55 ('looking for something (.) to comfort us/'). Coupled with his personal anecdotes, these non-fluency features reinforce Woo's sincerity in responding to Lees' question.

Part of the situational context of the exchange involves audience interaction. Aside from audience members, such as Lees, asking questions, it is also important that Jones and his panellists involve the audience present in the studio as much as possible, even if not directly addressing them. This can be seen with Woo's fast-paced aside '<A Jones and Couchman, if anyone appreciates that classic A>' (75), which is a tongue-in-cheek jab at Jones through reference to his father's mathematics textbook; the emphatic stress on 'classic' (75) in the subordinate clause 'if anyone appreciates that classic' is evidence of light-hearted sarcasm, as few people would appreciate textbooks from their schooling days. This banter reduces the social distance between Jones and Woo as it is the type of teasing that would typically occur between friends. The audience laughter in line 76 shows their involvement and appreciation of the gentle mockery. A reduced social distance is beneficial to the show as Australian audiences prefer to be entertained by amiable, teasing exchanges over formal, polite interactions.

In order to present his point of view as to what makes a good teacher, Woo uses coherent, logical ordering of ideas in his discussion of the difficulties people face in learning mathematics. He firstly reveals his own struggles with maths as a student in the referential 'I struggled with mathematics' (30) – and uses this first-person viewpoint to then speak on behalf of the Australian audience through the use of strong declaratives. These declaratives have emphatic stress firmly on negatively connoted adjectives that describe maths:

mathematics is 'hard\' (41) and 'abstract\' (42). The falling intonation placed on those adjectives also presents them as fact rather than opinion, allowing Woo to convincingly present the conclusion that people blame their lack of mathematical proficiency on abstract nouns such as 'genetics' (52) and 'society' (53) as it is a 'comfort' (55). Woo therefore fulfils his role as a panellist by constructing a meaningful, logical response to Lees' question.

While Woo's explanation of the feelings people hold towards mathematics is a relevant response to the question asked by Lees, it does not necessarily address the core topic of this episode of *Q+A*: that is, good teaching. As host, Jones therefore prompts Woo with the interrogative 'how is it that you can explain things that many other people struggle with?' (68–69) to create a coherent topic shift that allows Woo to present his opinion as to what makes a good teacher: 'I think that empathy is the key ingredient (.) of great teaching\' (85). The falling intonation used by Woo signals the end of his turn, and Jones responds to this cue by taking control of the floor, and of turn-taking, directing his next comments to another panellist, Cindy Berwick (90). This reinforces his role as host, as he must ensure that each panellist is given the opportunity to take a turn.

TIPS

- An important element of any spoken text is its prosodic features; ensure these are discussed throughout your analysis. Prosodic features are pitch, intonation, stress, volume and tempo.
- When discussing pauses as a prosodic feature, be careful to specify that you are analysing it as an aspect of the tempo. Additionally, be aware that some pauses may not be prosodic features but rather non-fluency features.
- While you are not expected to include every transcription symbol in the examples you quote, you should include any symbol that is relevant to your analysis.

TEXT N

Sample response

'The Hottest 100 has a new home' is a written online text, which has a referential function and promotional purpose regarding the Hottest 100 broadcast date change, aimed at triple j listeners. The ABC aims to justify the change and reaffirm its neutrality regarding the controversial date of Australia Day.

The register of this text, while mostly adhering to conventions of Standard Australian English, is somewhat informal, as the author has adopted a casual tenor to intimate familiarity with triple j's followers. Having said that, the text includes a range of formal features in keeping with a press release from the national broadcaster. Informally, the author refers to triple j listeners using the familiar, informal second-person pronoun 'you' numerous times (lines 2, 10, 53, 68), allowing the radio station to appear more familiar with the readers, encouraging them to be on side with the changes to a popular event. For example, in 'as voted by you' (4), the responsibility for the change is shifted onto the reader using the pronoun, ensuring they feel included but also discouraging resistance. Similarly, the text features a range of lexical choices that are not only relatively informal, but also convey aspects of triple j's identity as representative of Australian youth. These include the colloquial use of 'heaps' (line 8) and 'tonnes' (line 18) as quantitative adjectives to mean 'many'; the imitation of the spoken mode in the assimilated verb phrase 'gonna' (17), and the shortened name 'Caz' (line 50), which is a typical feature of Australian vocatives. The reference to 'Caz's pool' (line 50) is further evidence of an Australian identity, in that it reflects the typical Australian experience of spending time at a friend's pool during summer. These informal features position triple j as iconically Australian and imply that this remains the case, regardless of the date change. Despite these informal features, the text maintains an appropriate level of formality that befits a press release from the ABC. There are examples of elevated nouns in 'perspectives' (line 56) and 'questionnaire' (line 58) that add gravity and evidence to support the purpose of promoting the date change. The text mostly adheres to standard punctuation and spelling throughout, such as the simple sentence in line 1 that has both a capital letter to start and a full stop to end. It is noteworthy, however, that capital letters are not used when referring to 'triple j', in keeping with the station's branding and its desire to appear more casual. The carefully constructed conversational register functions to decrease the social distance between the radio station and the readers, thus supporting the promotional purpose.

The text's function is referential, informing readers that the Hottest 100 countdown has moved to the new date of 'Saturday 27 January 2018' (line 3). This is established in line 1 with the subheading 'The Hottest 100 has a new home'. This metaphorical declarative sentence immediately establishes the topic: that the Hottest 100's 'new home' will be a different date. The clear communication of this shift is reaffirmed throughout the text with repetition of the noun phrase 'fourth weekend of January' (lines 25 and 26). Syntax has an important role in the referential function throughout the text. Interrogatives are used in its subheadings, such as 'Why did you choose the fourth weekend of January?' (line 25) and 'What did people have to say ...?' (line 52), echoing readers' likely questions. These then allow the ABC to address these issues in the following lines using declaratives such as 'Your voice ... is as important as ours' in line 53, to fulfil the referential function. As this declarative also has a conative function, addressing the audience's strong feelings of needing to be heard, the promotional purpose is addressed here too.

The ABC also seeks to justify the date change to readers. Generalisations in the form of noun phrases such as 'heaps of you' (line 8), 'the majority of you' (lines 61–2) and 'most of you' (line 11) demonstrate the democratic nature of the decision. Furthermore, the author has included statistical and numerical data to prove that there were '64,990 responses [to the survey] to be precise' (line 58) and that '60%' of those were 'in favour of moving the Hottest 100 to a different date' (line 62). This not only reassures listeners that their views have been heard, but also helps to promote the values of the radio station, which aims to be representative of the people given it is the national broadcaster. Triple j also wants to appear mindful of its public perception and to reassure its followers that it is sensitive to public tensions surrounding Australia Day itself. The writer uses the modal verb 'should' in lines 45 and 46 – 'It should be an event that everyone can enjoy together' – to demonstrate that the cultural value of inclusivity holds greater significance than the controversy regarding Australia Day. The writer also ends this paragraph with the anaphoric, 'This is really important to us' (48), allowing the writer to demonstrate their inclusive values, which they hope are in line with those of their readers, who are drawn into the group in the following line with the subordinating conjunction and second-person pronoun 'Whether you're' (49). An alliterative list of familiar and common Australian places such 'Busselton, Bundy ... backyard BBQ' (49–50) and the nouns 'everyone' and 'party' (51) create the sense of inclusion and build solidarity with the audience.

Section C: Sustained expository response

Mark allocation: 30 marks

- Section C is marked holistically based on the criteria provided by VCAA.

TIPS

- Often questions in Section C begin with a small quotation and then the question itself. Students often miss the question, providing a response that focuses on the quotation only and is therefore inappropriate. For example, if a question asks you to consider the 'extent' to which the statement is true, it requires an opinion to be expressed on the initial statement. In contrast, a 'Discuss' question requires a balanced exploration of the statement.
- Your response must clearly address the topic. At the beginning and end of each paragraph, double-check your topic sentence and linking sentence to ensure you are still answering the question asked.
- Your main body paragraphs should be structured to respond directly to the topic. Ensure your paragraphs are well structured, with clear topic sentences, explanations, evidence and linking sentences.
- In your response, you must include reference to the stimulus; this is part of the marking criteria. That being said, avoid referring to every piece of stimulus in your response, as this does not allow you to demonstrate depth of knowledge or your own independent reasoning and examples.
- Contemporary examples from media and society are strongly encouraged and will form a part of any high-scoring response. Be careful, however, to avoid discussing the issues themselves – the focus is on how language is used in society, not on what happened or how people react to events or controversies.
- Recent and relevant examples of language use are preferred over dated or unoriginal evidence. Be aware that the following sample responses contain examples from the years they were originally written – your examples should all be drawn from current discussion and debate.
- Pre-prepared or generic responses are strongly discouraged; they are easily detected, and it is very difficult for these types of responses to achieve a high score.
- Ensure you include metalanguage in your response, particularly when referring to contemporary examples. It is important that you show a deep understanding of the metalanguage specific to the course; generalised discussions are not rewarded.

Question 1

'From social media to international media to the proliferation of online gaming, the internet is clearly having an impact on language whether we like it or not.'

Discuss with reference to contemporary Australian society. Refer to at least **two** subsystems of language in your response.

Possible approaches

This topic requires a discussion of how the internet has changed the way we use language. Students can discuss a range of contexts where this has happened. The last part of the question invites a discussion of attitudes towards these changes. There are opportunities with this question to explore changing trends in relation to language in social media and globalised media such as news and entertainment. This would also consider those who use this language as an expression of identity and the power of internet speak in conveying information that crosses into real life. Therefore, key knowledge from all areas of study will be relevant for this topic.

Responses could explore any of the following:

- awareness of how language has specifically changed in relation to neologisms and changing semantics, and therefore increased rates of acceptance of variation
- innovation of language and how it has adapted over time as new technology and values emerge
- how identity is expressed or shaped through language online
- government speak online in relation to social issues or current events
- the ease with which we can communicate to more people more often, and how this impacts our language use, with communication becoming more informal in many contexts
- the association between online language and age- or activity-based sociolects
- generational sociolects and prejudice between groups based on language choices
- the impact of worldwide variations in English on Australian English.

Sample response

The internet has changed the way we use language in a range of contexts in contemporary Australian society. We can communicate with more people more frequently, which means new terms are entering English rapidly, and existing lexical items are being repurposed to reflect trends and societal changes or attitudes. With access to a range of news, entertainment and social media platforms, professionals and members of the public are using the internet to construct identities or share their views. Some view these changes favourably, but others see the detrimental effects of the globalisation of information on Australian English.

The globalised sharing of entertainment, news and community has had a marked impact on Australian English. The internet has given rise to a plethora of new terms that have been introduced to the English language. These terms are being used across the globe by people of different age groups and organisations, with many moving from the written to the spoken mode. Non-standard terms such as 'noob' (Stimulus C), 'lewk' and 'finsta' are popular on gaming sites and Instagram with the younger generation. They are also now being uttered in day-to-day conversations, with *lewk* being pronounced with emphatic stress on the /ʉː/ phoneme when saying /lʉːk/ instead of the more standard pronunciation /lʊk/ in Australia. These terms create an in-group of users, who are expressing their identity as young people. Acronyms and initialisms are also commonplace online, with new ones appearing all the time. Examples are LMIRL (let's meet in real life) and DM (direct message), which are used on social media platforms such as Snapchat, Reddit, WhatsApp and Facebook and in online gaming chat. These abbreviations are utilised not only by younger people, but also by large organisations. On Macquarie Bank's Twitter page in January 2021, it posted 'DM me' in response to a customer, to arrange to have a member of its team discuss mortgages. Using this language, the organisation comes across as more personable and acceptable on an online platform (Stimulus A). Furthermore, while many Australians will still doggedly update the language on their Microsoft applications to allow 'colour' and 'neighbour' to be spelled with an 'ou' instead of the American 'color' or 'neighbor', it is an uphill battle. As David Astle points out (Stimulus D), our steady diet of both scripted and unscripted entertainment from the US means that Australians are using Americanisms such as the colloquialism 'my bad' and the abbreviation '24/7' without even noting their origins. The internet has impacted our language because it links us to other communities of English speakers and because new terms are being created and used by people from all sectors of society.

The internet has also influenced the English language by appropriating existing vocabulary, often reflecting what is happening in our society. Denotations of lexical items commonly used in English have broadened as they are given new meanings in an online context. The noun 'troll' is no longer just a folklore creature; it has broadened to refer to a person who intentionally upsets others by posting inflammatory comments online. 'To troll' is an imperative verb with negative connotations as it is the action of writing these unpleasant comments online. In 2020 the Macquarie Dictionary, an authority on Australian English, declared 'Karen' and 'Covidiot' as the people's choice for words of the year. 'Karen', once a feminine proper noun, has broadened to become a pejorative slang term to label a person as entitled or abusing their privilege. It features regularly online in memes and to label women captured in viral videos engaging in mostly racist acts. 'Covidiot' came about as a blend of 'COVID-19' and 'idiot', to define someone refusing to follow the health advice and panic-buying during the pandemic in 2020. These slang terms spread quickly across the world through online communication, reflecting some sense of solidarity towards unfavourable acts in society. However, sometimes these language changes can offend or be taken out of context. Suppose someone disagrees with the opinions of another person and utilises a comment section to disagree with them. In that case, they might be incorrectly labelled as a 'troll', and there are Karens in the world who are not happy that their name is now synonymous with a bigoted white woman. Therefore, the internet has allowed us to give new meanings to existing words and phrases that quickly catch on across the globe and reflect common views on important issues; however, some of this language change is not viewed favourably by all members of our society.

Online communication has allowed organisations and people in positions of power to express a more informal identity as they incorporate linguistic innovation in their public personas. Former Australian prime minister Scott Morrison uses the informal blend 'ScoMo' in his Facebook handle, and current Prime Minister Anthony Albanese has shortened his surname, so he is 'AlboMP' on X (formerly known as Twitter). Both use hashtags, another feature of social media and online communication, to connect their content to specific topics, events, themes or conversations, such as #Straya. On the Victoria Police's Instagram page, 'doggo' (a popular internet term) was used in a pun-filled post captioned 'We asked Champ to help us hoomans be better at mask wearing. He took this impawtant task very seriously'. Some comments featured masked face and dog emojis, another unique feature of internet chat that has changed how we communicate, adding emotion or humour or a substitute for body language in the written mode. By using informal language as part of their online media presence, politicians and organisations can convey a more casual identity, to whom the public can relate. It reduces the social distance between the people in positions of power, which is viewed favourably in an Australian cultural context with egalitarian values. These individuals and organisations have embraced online communication. They have set up social media pages to connect with the public while still understanding the need for more formal language in other contexts – as is expected considering their roles in society.

Online communication, news and entertainment has enabled greater and faster communication in our lives. It has also changed the way that members of our society use language – mostly for the good, even though it is never possible to please everyone. Online communication is a means for linguistic innovation. We can use it to display or create certain identities, and it often reflects issues in today's modern world.

Question 2

'Language has important societal purposes, and it fosters feelings of both group identity and solidarity.'

Discuss, referring to at least **two** subsystems of language in your response.

Possible approaches

When responding to this question, note the importance of 'both'. If you explore only group identity or only solidarity, you won't fully address the question. Given the instruction word is 'Discuss', it is less appropriate to consider how language can be used to create disharmony as an antonym to solidarity; although this is true, the question would ask 'to what extent' if it invited disagreement. You might consider alternative societal purposes, however. You should acknowledge contextual factors and explore individual and group identity in your response; you need to show you understand that through our language we express ourselves as individuals and signal our membership of particular groups. Though this topic appears to lean more towards Unit 4 – Language variation and identity, you can examine language in contemporary Australian social settings, along a continuum of informal and formal contexts.

Responses could explore any of the following:

- the use of Standard Australian English, and how it differs from other English varieties
- the features of Broad, General and Cultivated Australian English accents, and how these sound different from other English varieties
- the cultural varieties of Australian English that are unique to Australia, such as migrant ethnolects and Aboriginal Australian Englishes
- geographical differences, including national and regional
- the relationship between context and the features of language with regard to social situations and cultural expectations
- the role of language in reflecting, establishing and challenging different identities
- how a sense of identity evolves in response to situations and experiences and is influenced by how we see ourselves and how others see us.

Sample response

Language is the means by which we know ourselves and our place in the society around us. As such, it serves a range of important societal purposes – building and reflecting group identity and demonstrating our participation in Australian society. Language is a significant indicator that reflects the social groups individuals belong to and aspects of their cultural identity and Australia's national identity. It fosters a sense of belonging and group identity that helps build solidarity in society, to maintain social harmony. Language enables us to reflect our belief in Australian values, such as the doctrine of egalitarianism and a 'fair go' for all. At a personal level, language provides indicators of being part of an ethno-cultural group or identifies users according to age, interests and occupation.

Australians are identifiable to each other by the uniqueness of the accent and lexis of the country, which connects them both socially and culturally. Accent is a key determiner in placing where a person is from; in Australia, many of us sound similar, as the General accent is used by 'a vast majority of Australians' (Karl Quinn, *Sydney Morning Herald*, August 2021). This sameness also supports the notion that egalitarianism is valued in our culture. The distinctive Australian vowels are a significant indicator, with the /ɑe/ phoneme sounding more like /oɪ/ and the assimilation of /t/ to /d/. Dave Speers, an Australian journalist and host of the television news and discussion program *ABC Insiders*, does not dilute his Australian accent when reporting on important issues or interviewing politically powerful individuals. When speaking with Anne Ruston, then Minister for Women's Safety, he spoke of using /ˈtwɪdə/ (Twitter) and drawing the /loɪn/ (line). In addition to the accent, Australians tend to be informal in speech, using unique colloquialisms and shortenings. Greeting friends or strangers with the informal colloquial phrase 'G'day, mate' might seem stereotypical but it is still used in many contexts in this country. On their podcast *All Day Breakfast*, hosts Matt Okine and Alex Dyson frequently greet listeners of their 'poddie' (a typically informal Australian example of a shortening with a hypocoristic suffix). Similarly, former prime minister Scott Morrison claimed to greet the French President with a 'G'day' at the G20 summit. In addition, during COVID-19 pressers to the Victorian people in 2021, the Victorian Premier regularly reflected his informal Australian identity with a range of shortenings, including 'iso' and 'ambo'. With a positive attitude towards the accent and unique colloquial language, Australian English is an important marker of identity both socially and culturally, used by the majority of Australians to build a national identity and maintain an egalitarian and harmonious society.

Another marker of identity in the Australian context is the range of culturally specific varieties being used across the country, including ethnolects and Aboriginal Australian Englishes (AAE). These varieties carry covert prestige as they enable their users to express their membership of particular social groups and reflect their cultural identity. One of the ethnolects used in Australia is the Greek-Australian ethnolect. I have a friend who is second-generation Australian with Greek grandparents. When in the company of other Greek-Australians, her ethnolect becomes more apparent: she decentralises the /æ/ vowel to /e/ as in 'have', and affricates the /t/ phoneme to a /ts/ in lexemes such as 'that'. Similarly, Australian Greens politician and Gunnai, Gunditjmara and Djab Wurrung woman Lidia Thorpe uses Aboriginal English on her social media, such as the non-Standard spelling of 'Blak' in many of her posts and the reference to 'deadly sistergirls and brotherboys' in her Trans Awareness Week Twitter post in November 2021. The adjective 'deadly', with its positive connotation, is common among AAE users, and the compound nouns for trans individuals are used in Aboriginal communities and thus these terms help Thorpe build solidarity with her constituents. As well as creating a sense of in-group with other First Nations peoples, Thorpe is overtly reflecting her identity as Aboriginal. Her use of AAE on a platform that reaches people outside her community shows that, culturally in Australia, we are becoming more accepting of these non-Standard varieties used by people in this social group. Cultural language varieties are thus 'distinguishing markers of social identity' (Burridge and De Laps), playing a significant role in strengthening cultural identity in Australia, especially when used in the public domain.

Language use can vary depending on social context, with different sociolects being used as a means of expressing one's identity in relation to age or occupation. By adhering to the language conventions when in the company of these social groups, individuals establish and mark their in-group identity due to their shared identity with this crowd. Teenagers identify their social standing by using teen speak, which is often innovative and informal. 'Tmr we runnin back sum exams on site' is typical of language used by young people, with shortenings of lexical items and non-Standard spelling and semantic changes. The Australian Federal Police capitalised on this, using up-to-date slang to target young Australians in the lead-up to Black Friday sales, warning them that 'y'all Gen Z be no cap most likely to fall for the scammers' (Stimulus C), using the popular slang 'no cap' to mean 'truthfully'. This addresses the important social function of community safety, by using in-group language in an unusual context to build solidarity with this group. Occupational speak, though generally more formal, can also indicate that an individual belongs to a particular social group. Medical jargon such as 'serology' and 'immunosorbent assay' allows medical professionals to project an identity of expertise and academia by portraying their depth of knowledge and reflecting their identity as someone who works in this field. In both instances, the language being used in context is a marker of identity in a social setting, and culturally, in Australia, there is an expectation that speakers will use the 'right' language to fit in with their social groups, though this can be subverted for effect. As such, language is adapted for varied purposes and reflects different aspects of shared identities.

In contemporary Australian society, language is a marker of social aspects of identity as well as cultural aspects of identity. With most Australians sounding similar, we identify as part of this nation, but we can also reflect more specific social aspects of our identities by using language that reflects our cultural background, age or occupation. These identities help the country to build a harmonious society.

Question 3

'Australia is a multicultural country, but its inhabitants must conform to language norms in order to fit in.'

To what extent is this true in contemporary Australian society? Refer to at least **two** subsystems of language in your response.

Possible approaches

When responding to this question, it is essential to note the modal verb 'must' and to address the directive 'To what extent is this true?' For this topic, consider language norms in Australian society. This might include the Australian preference for more casual language and shortenings with suffixation. That said, there has been a clear shift to other Australian Englishes being more prominent in public domains, such as Aboriginal Australian Englishes and migrant ethnolect varieties, which must be addressed in your response given the description of Australia in the question as 'multicultural'. Attitudes towards these varieties have changed over time but there are some in Australian society who might still view them as not quintessentially 'Aussie'. You may also consider that context determines what language is considered the norm and acceptable. High-scoring responses will explore the multifaceted nature of our identities, and the way we change our language to suit the setting and our audience.

Responses could explore any of the following:

- the features of Australian English accents, including Broad, General and Cultivated accents
- the role of Standard English and other varieties of English in Australian society
- the characteristics of Australian English, in contrast to Englishes from other continents, including phonological, morphological, lexical and grammatical patterns
- the features of language that contribute to a sense of national identity from across the subsystems
- how the language of individuals and the language of groups are shaped by social expectations and community attitudes
- how culture can influence varieties of Australian English, including Aboriginal Australian Englishes and migrant ethnolects
- the relationship between language choices and social attitudes towards different varieties of Australian English.

Sample response

When it comes to language norms and fitting in, context plays a large role in what is considered acceptable language use in Australia. There is certainly some expectation that Australian speakers know and understand Standard Australian English as well as some of the colloquialisms used in this country, but often it is the way a person speaks rather than the words they use that helps them 'fit in'. However, attitudes about what Australian English looks and sounds like are changing, and there is growing acceptance of cultural varieties even in the public domain. Language norms also vary according to situational and cultural factors, so each person accommodates their language to fit in with these. Therefore, while there might be some language norms we conform to, language norms are changing on a broader scale and can also shift depending on the context of the situation.

In Australia, there is some presumption that citizens and residents will know terms unique to the country that are standardised, and also some of the informal, colloquial language that is regarded so highly. That said, it is not just the terminology people use that makes them fit in, it is the way those words sound. The importance of being able to use English proficiently is apparent, with the Australian Department of Home Affairs making changes to the Adult Migrant English Program, offering migrants with low English levels a service to improve their English language skills. The department states on its official website that, 'Learning English will help you to participate more fully in Australian life ... [and to] work and make friends.' In addition to this, other more formal organisations such as the Australian Broadcasting Corporation (ABC), and less formal organisations such as the *Aussie English* podcast by Pete Smissen, offer learning opportunities for newly arrived Australians, providing information on topics such as parenting a toddler 'when English is your second language' or the meaning of the colloquial phrase 'as thick as thieves'. However, being able to use nouns such as 'thongs' and 'doona' in the right context, or knowing that the discourse particle 'yeah nah' means 'no', does not necessarily mean you are using language norms that help you fit in. My father moved to Australia as an adult from England, and despite using these terms in his day-to-day discourse, he never fitted in as an 'Aussie' because he could not shift his English accent. So, when he uttered the typical informal greeting of 'How's it going, mate?' he didn't assimilate the final –g, nor did he elongate the –a, and therefore his 'Britishness' was still very apparent. Hence, knowing how to use Australian English might help someone to fit in but it does not necessarily mean they will be viewed as fully Australian.

More inclusively, in recent years there has been a positive attitude shift towards Aboriginal Australian Englishes (AAE) and ethnic varieties of Australian English, both of which are not used by the general public but in smaller speech communities. Italian-Australian comedian Joe Avati presents his comedy using his Italian-Australian ethnolect. In his TikTok videos he mentions his family from 'Italy' /ɪtəliː/ but with his ethnolect, it sounds more like /ˈɪtəːliː/ with the elongated vowel sound in the middle. Ethnolect speakers like Avati adapt features of their cultural native language to Australian English in order to reflect an identity and fit in with other ethnolect users; they are also accepted in Australian society as Australian but with a slightly ethnic aspect. In addition, the Victorian Government COVIDSafe DH Vaccine Ticket Campaign included the line, 'And to the perfectly brewed tea and advice you've missed with your Yiayia'. The noun 'Yiayia' is borrowed from Greek, but it is so commonplace in multicultural Australia that it was used in an advertisement aimed at all Victorians. Similarly, Aboriginal Australian Englishes are being used more frequently in the public domain, with characters in the ABC program *Preppers* using AAE, such as the adjective 'deadly' with its positive connotation, and the noun 'gammin', meaning fake or pretend (Stimulus B). The semantics of these terms are known more generally in Australia now and do not need translating for non–First Nations peoples. Linguistic norms have shifted, and it is now normal to see or hear a range of cultural varieties of English in Australia, suggesting our values see multiculturalism as the best fit for the country.

Context also influences language norms, and language can change remarkably from one context to another. In most instances, humans are adept at knowing what language norms are appropriate in particular situations; if they do not adhere to those norms, they might be viewed unfavourably. In Australia we are not only inclusive of people of different ethnic and cultural backgrounds – at the heart of Australian culture are values of respect and fairness, and our overt language norms demonstrate these values. The Australian Government Style Manual promotes 'language that is culturally appropriate and respectful of the diversity of Australia's peoples'. We see groups and individuals showing that they take on board these values, such as BankVic using the gender-neutral noun 'Chair' for its presiding officer and Healthdirect Australia referring to 'gender confirmation surgery' – 'confirmation' has a more positive connotation than the formerly used term, 'reassignment'. When groups or individuals break these cultural norms there is often a backlash, such as when the NRL investigated player James Tedesco over an alleged racial slur towards a woman of Vietnamese background. The sister of the victim stated that it might 'seem like a joke' to Tedesco but as a person in a position of authority and a role model, his 'joke' is not considered amusing. In a different vein, former Victorian Chief Health Officer Brett Sutton demonstrated how context influences his language. When introduced at a press conference by then-Minister for Health Martin Foley, Sutton said, 'Thank you, Minister' – a politeness marker and honorific. However, when addressing the Victorian public, he used 'Vic' and 'Shep' – shortening place names. In the first instance, Sutton met the face needs of a person in a position of authority, whereas in the second instance he used more casual language that appealed to the general public. In both instances Sutton adhered to language norms to fit in with a particular context. Language norms mean more than just conforming to the stereotypical 'laid-back' Australian identity in order to fit in; they mean understanding the country's cultural values and using the appropriate language accordingly. Additionally, situational context is important, and the right language needs to be used to fit in with different contexts.

Australia is a multicultural country with a variety of Australian Englishes used; however, it also has a shared national identity that reflects the values of inclusion and acceptance. Australians also understand that context plays a major role when it comes to language norms and fitting in, and that this might mean being more formal in some contexts and less so in others.

Question 4

'Australian English is changing, as it must. And these changes should be welcomed.'

To what extent is this true in contemporary Australia? Refer to at least **two** subsystems of language in your response.

Possible approaches

When planning a response to this question, students must take note of the directive 'To what extent is this true ...?' Students need to consider how much they agree or disagree that Australian English *must* change. They are also expected to consider how much they agree or disagree with the second part of this prompt, which suggests that change should be welcomed. They need to be able to explain how language change does or does not weaken or impair Australian English but enhances it for a range of reasons. Students' understanding should be made clear in the introduction and restated in the conclusion.

Students should aim to include key knowledge from across Units 3 and 4 when responding to this prompt in order to demonstrate their scope of understanding of the course. Higher-scoring responses will acknowledge that through language we communicate information about our values and attitudes, and that language allows us to communicate facets of our identity. Students will also recognise that Standard Australian English is still granted prestige in contemporary Australian society, and that it has a role in establishing national identity through its unique lexicon and colloquialisms.

Responses could explore any of the following:

- how non-discriminatory language aims to uphold the respect and acceptance of minority groups
- how language change occurs alongside social movements that champion the use of inclusive language to support marginalised groups
- how we are more inclined to employ politeness strategies, euphemisms and all-encompassing language to meet face needs
- how language has changed as Australian values have changed
- how Australia is accepting of other dialects and varieties, as exemplified through ethnolects and Aboriginal Australian Englishes, as well as First Nations languages being recognised in public contexts
- the influence of online platforms, with textspeak being fairly uniform globally – this could include references to the influences of other Englishes, such as aspects of American English and British English
- how some aspects of Australian English will not change as Standard Australian English reflects a shared national identity, and informality through the use of colloquial language is still valued in mainstream society
- how Stimulus A could suggest that using traditional First Nations names for places both acknowledges and celebrates the connection of First Nations peoples to those places and may lead to a more accepting Australian society
- how Stimulus B shows that diversity in Australia is exemplified through language, with the figures using terms of greetings from the Aussie 'G'day' to borrowings such as the Italian 'ciao'
- how Stimulus C and Stimulus D show that cultural language varieties are becoming more prevalent in mainstream society, with a First Nations senator using the non-Standard spelling of 'Blak' and the noun 'mob' on a public platform, and familial terms like the Greek 'yiayia' and Italian 'nonna' being often used by descendants of migrants.

Sample response

Language in Australia is changing, and it is important that it does so, in order to reflect modern views and values held by most Australians. The rise of non-discriminatory language validates marginalised groups in our society, making them feel included. Additionally, shifting attitudes towards the use of cultural varieties in Australia, particularly in mainstream and public language, shows that Australians are more accepting of migrant communities and First Nations peoples. Though some may argue that changes to Australian English are detrimental, the changes we are seeing occur alongside the idea of a 'traditional' Australian language. This ensures that a sense of national identity is maintained but that Australians are also progressive and welcome language change that reflects our inclusive and accepting society.

In modern Australia, language users are more aware of the need to employ inclusive and non-discriminatory language. Such language is more accurate, fair and respectful, which reflects contemporary social values. In 2022, the Moreland City Council officially changed its name to 'Merri-bek' (rocky country), and a local Melbourne high school named their new building 'wilam-nganjin' (our place). Community members in both instances generally supported the use of the Woi-wurrung language for these public institutions. Replacing European names or choosing to use Indigenous languages can be a positive move towards reconciliation. The use of these traditional First Nations names publicly acknowledges and celebrates the connection of First Nations peoples to these places and the land on which we work and study (Stimulus A). This illustrates that by welcoming language change in mainstream and public settings, society's attitudes towards becoming more inclusive and accepting may change as well.

An understanding of language and gender is another more recent shift that makes people feel seen and valued. High-profile politicians, such as Senator Penny Wong, display their pronouns on their social media pages. This is a public show that they acknowledge the importance of pronouns when it comes to each person's identity. It is a small but significant way to invite members of a community to share their gender pronouns, making them feel welcome and seen in modern society. The high-profile examples can pave the way for other Australians to add their pronoun to their email signature, or to ask a new acquaintance 'What are your pronouns?', building this into a new norm. In addition, the ACT Government introduced gender-neutral language in a range of laws and regulations in the territory, substituting references to binary genders in favour of 'they', 'their', 'them', 'themselves' or relevant nouns such as 'Attorney-General'. The use of gender-neutral language is important to create an accepting and inclusive society in which all community members are included. By welcoming more inclusive language, society seeks to treat all people with respect, dignity and impartiality. Thus, language change can be important and powerful when creating an inclusive and welcoming community.

Where in the past, ethnolects and Aboriginal Australian Englishes (AAE) were mostly contained within those cultural groups, changing attitudes around the acceptance and understanding of other Englishes has seen these varieties enter the mainstream, enriching the language of Australia. AAEs are seen and heard in a range of contexts, such as on the social media pages of notable First

Nations people: for example, Senator Lidia Thorpe posted a non-standardised form of spelling of 'Blak' and the familial noun 'mob' in an Instagram post in November 2022 (Stimulus C). Darwin's Ben Graetz, the creative director of Sydney WorldPride, was interviewed by ABC Online in December 2022 and stated that the event would be 'deadly' and that he was looking forward to celebrating his 'brotherboy and sistergirl' community. This is AAE being used on a global platform, without Graetz even having to explain the meaning of these terms as they are widely understood. Due to Australia's multicultural identity, in many local communities, familial nouns such as the Greek 'yiayia' and Italian 'nonna' are understood by Australians who are not part of this ethnic background. The comedian Mary Coustas uses her Greek-Australian ethnolect as a major part of her comedy. When advertising her upcoming tour as character Effie Stephanidis on her Facebook page, Coustas showcases Effie's Greek-Australian ethnolect. She opens the video with 'Hello', whereby the sound production of the fricative /h/ moves further to the back of the throat. She follows this with the politeness marker 'Thanks', in which, with the final phoneme, /s/ is substituted with /ʃ/. The pluralisation of the second-person pronoun 'you' to 'youse' is also a feature of her character's language. As this ethnic dialect is well known, even outside of the Greek-Australian community, the humour around Effie's language is embedded into Australian culture and therefore appeals to a broad Australian audience. AAE, ethnolects and codeswitching should be welcomed in order to reflect the changing nature of Australian identity and communities.

While it is necessary that we accept changes to the language of Australia, undoubtedly there are aspects of Australian English that are unlikely to significantly alter over time. Standard Australian English, colloquial language and the Australian accent are strong markers of national identity and distinguish Australian English from other Englishes. Australians understand the semantics of lexemes such as the nouns 'doona' and 'bogan'. They also understand how to shorten and add hypocoristic suffixes to create terms such as 'postie' and 'servo'. Colloquialisms such as the greeting 'g'day' and the phrase 'bloody ripper' are also seen and heard in a range of contexts. Even politicians and news sources employ the more casual language Australians are known for, such as when South Australian Minister for Health and Wellbeing, the Hon Chris Picton MP, stated, 'We have ended the Liberals' war on our ambos'. In addition, Australian senior correspondent Nick Bryant has used *Journo* as the title of his news and current affairs podcast. These very public instances of 'Aussie' language from people in positions of authority reinforce that it is part of the national identity. In addition, the way Australians sound has not changed greatly over time, with most of the population speaking with the General accent. This is stated to be 'uniquely Australian' by Macquarie University and it can create a sense of in-group membership and pride. For example, referring to the conversations had at the Sydney WorldPride Human Rights Conference in 2023, Australian performer Courtney Act stated on their podcast *Brenda, Call Me!*, 'it's really nice to speak all of those conversations with an Australian accent ... because it's <u>our</u> voice'. So, while Australian English is changing to an extent, some aspects are relatively unchanged and 'colloquialisms ... are like accents – part of the glue that sticks Australian English speakers together' (ABC, January 2023).

> It is evident that Australian English has changed and will continue to change. These changes have come about due to shifting attitudes towards inclusive language, which comes in the form of non-discriminatory terminology and greater acceptance of new varieties of Australian English. Nevertheless, some aspects have stood the test of time and are universally identified as uniquely Australian. Change is welcomed and accepted by most in contemporary Australia, with some aspects of the dialects, such as vocabulary, grammar and pronunciation, still being unique to Australia and Australians.

Question 5

'Informal language forms an integral part of the Australian national identity.'

Discuss, referring to at least **two** subsystems of language in your response.

Possible approaches

As this is a 'Discuss' question, students only need to consider aspects of informality. The question does not invite them to disagree or say to what extent, so formality is not particularly relevant here. Instead, the thesis should consider the Australian national identity and consider the integral aspects of informality. This will require drawing primarily upon Unit 3 Outcome 1 and Unit 4.

Responses could explore any of the following:

- how informal language can be more effective than a formal register as it is expressive and more relatable for many Australians
- that Australians in public positions consider how their messages will be interpreted and understand that informal language is granted more overt prestige in many contexts
- how emojis can impact the informality of a text, with many Australians using them to add pragmatic features to a written form
- how shared informal language supports in-group membership among all Australians, regardless of where they have come from or where their ancestors have come from
- how non-Standard and other informal language is inclusive, light-hearted and establishes rapport, which are all valued in Australia and something many strive to achieve
- how Stimulus A supports the idea that informal language is inclusive and mutually understood among Australians; many Australians pride themselves on their unique variety of English and it helps create a sense of national pride and identity
- how Stimulus B asserts that aspects of informal language in Australia are integral to feeling and being viewed as Australian
- how Stimulus C shows how linguistic innovation and terms of affection in the form of nicknames are valued in Australian society and that these are used by organisations to appeal to the public
- how Stimulus D illustrates how non-Standard informal language from other Australian English varieties are more accepted by the broader community.

Sample response

Australians have long been known for their casual and relaxed attitude, and this reputation has come about partly due to the informal language often used in conversation. Informal colloquialisms and phonological features are prevalent throughout society and used by various people in a wide range of contexts, including by politicians and journalists. Australians are also known for their colourful and innovative language, which is not intended to offend but acts as an agent to convey a sense of in-group membership and mateship or to intensify a particular sentiment. Australia is a proudly multicultural country, and this value is firmly entrenched in the national identity embraced by many Australians. Language from various ethnic and cultural groups is considered informal but also important for those wanting to express this facet of their identity.

Informal language is seen and heard all over Australia, from households to workplaces and in public contexts including politics and news broadcasting. It is not uncommon to come across colloquialisms and informal phonological processes such as vowel reductions and assimilation in these contexts. Nowadays, public figures such as politicians often use relatively informal language to build rapport and gain favour with voters. For example, Prime Minister Anthony Albanese posted 'Saturday arvo with Toto' and 'Brekky in Melbourne' on his Instagram page. These shortenings with hypocoristic suffixation, 'arvo' and 'Brekky', are a common feature of Australian English, and by using these, Albanese is showing he is relatable and aligns himself with the more laid-back national identity. The rapport-building function of such slang terms is also seen in Stimulus B, where Evan Kidd suggests that 'using Australian slang increases your likeability'. Network 10 journalist Narelda Jacobs also aligns herself with mainstream society when she assimilates verbs such as 'going' by converting the /ŋ/ final phoneme to /n/ and when she voices the /t/ in the noun 'Saturday' as /d/. Both these sounds in connected speech are used by everyday Australians, and this modification to more informal speech is acceptable for members of our society to use, including prominent figures such as Jacobs. Thus, the use of casual language and speech is employed in a range of contexts, including traditionally formal ones, indicating that positive attitudes towards the role of informal language in the national identity have begun to supersede convention.

It is not uncommon to encounter colourful and innovative language from members of Australian society as it is often seen as a way to express mateship and inclusiveness, which are valued aspects of the national identity. Associate Professor Amanda Laugesen, Director of the Australian National Dictionary Centre at ANU, stated that 'colourful language [has] been called part of our national identity ... we [are] considered a nation that loves swear words'. Swear words considered taboo in some English-speaking contexts are not viewed that way in Australia, which is why companies and organisations will use the intensifier 'bloody' in their advertising and as part of their online presence. Hearing 'bloody' in Aussie Broadband's tagline, 'bloody good broadband', reinforces the company's identity as quintessentially Australian. Similarly, group fitness organisation Body Fit Training referred to their members as 'bloody legends' in a Facebook post in February 2023. Laugesen writes that 'bloody was ubiquitous in Australia' as early as 1847 according to Alexander Marjoribanks, who described it as 'the great Australian adjective', rather than a dysphemistic term. In addition, Australians reflect their larrikin identity through language such as unique idioms and rhyming slang. Comedian Matt Okine regularly uses 'what a Barry', in reference to Barry Crocker, to mean 'shocker' when something bad happens. This type of linguistic innovation showcases the larrikin identity that many value as uniquely Australian. Informal language in the form of expletives and colourful phrases is not meant to offend but instead to create a sense of solidarity as a nation and a way to exhibit a more laissez-faire and playful attitude towards language.

Ethnolects and Aboriginal Australian Englishes (AAE) are varieties of English used in Australia today that have informal elements. These dialects are integral in our society as they represent the multicultural facet of the Australian national identity. My mother's family originated from Italy and they feel their ethnolect is much more accepted in mainstream society these days. They will overtly use terms such as the noun 'bambini' to refer to the younger members of our family and use Italian-Australian suffixation so that 'farm' becomes 'farma' and 'cake' becomes 'keka'. Their pronunciation also differs from mainstream Australia as the politeness marker 'please' sounds more like 'pliss'. Similarly, on *The Voice Australia*, Jessica Mauboy asked First Nations performers Castlereagh Connection, 'where you mob actually come from?', and rapper/radio presenter Nooky uttered 'they be from Naarm' when referring to a fellow Aboriginal artist on his radio program on triple j. The use of AAE terms, such as Mauboy using the familial noun 'mob' in her interrogative, and the non-Standard syntax in Nooky's declarative, indicate that informal language can be used to reflect identity and a sense of in-group status within various cultural groups. With these various informal language varieties being used in public contexts, it is clear that non-Standard language used in informal contexts not only reflects one's identity but is also received more positively by the wider community. While these examples are currently considered informal, as these dialects become more and more prevalent, their non-Standard features will likely be used increasingly formally. This fits with Australia's national identity, being one that values inclusion and celebrates its multicultural community.

Informal language is typical across Australia and used in many contexts – so much so that it helps bind members of Australian society together and is thus a vital element in moulding our national identity.

Question 6

'Euphemisms are necessary in both formal and informal contexts.'

To what extent does this apply to contemporary Australian society? Refer to at least **two** subsystems of language in your response.

Possible approaches

This topic requires students to draw primarily on their understanding of Unit 3 Outcome 2, as well as some understanding of Outcome 1. Students should demonstrate an understanding of the place that euphemisms have in helping to maintain social harmony and navigating taboo topics within contemporary Australian society, including why people use them, how they are used and what impact they have on face needs and clarity of information. It would also be acceptable for students to provide some consideration of dysphemisms as a point of comparison, so long as this does not steer them too far away from the original topic – that being to assess the necessity of euphemisms in both formal and informal contexts. It is also important that students distinguish between contextual factors in the formulation of their response.

The stimuli invite students to discuss the way that euphemistic language can be used to make political comments in order to lessen offence; to consider how 'correct' non-discriminatory language actually is; to discuss the ways in which institutions change their language in order to appear more sensitive to the needs of the people they are advocates for, such as those in aged-care facilities; and to consider how corporate industries use euphemistic language to tackle uncomfortable topics, such as firing employees.

Responses might consider the following:

- how euphemisms are intended to navigate taboo and help maintain social harmony
- the role of euphemisms in formal contexts
- the role of euphemisms in informal contexts
- euphemisms in Australia's contemporary debates, as well as the ways that politicians use language to carry out their own agenda (double speak, obfuscation, exaggeration)
- informal use of euphemisms, such as anecdotal or personal examples for death, bodily functions, bodily fluids, sexual intercourse
- euphemisms that aid the communication of discriminatory views.

Sample response

Love them or hate them, euphemisms are a necessity in successful communication between people and groups in Australian society. While to some they may appear to obfuscate uncomfortable topics, they do serve an important purpose in allowing topics that are seen to be taboo or sensitive to be discussed without offence. The primary purpose of euphemistic language is to maintain social harmony while providing speakers with a lexicon that allows them to navigate social contexts and their varying expectations. There is some argument that more formal contexts demand more euphemistic language; however, there is a place for euphemisms in both informal and formal communication.

Euphemisms can provide speakers with more non-discriminatory language that can assist in the maintenance of social harmony by avoiding offence. This is often the case when discussing sensitive topics such as race or racial discrimination, as seen in Stimulus A, where Osamah Sami made the observation that he was only on the stage assisting in the presentation of an award so that the AACTA could 'fulfil the diversity quota'. Use of the noun phrase 'the diversity quota', rather than directly saying something such as, 'I am here because I have brown skin', allowed Sami to make his point that the Australian film and television industry 'doesn't care about diversity' without causing undue discomfort to those watching. Similarly, at funerals, which have both formal and informal aspects, rather than using direct and abrasive phrases such as 'sorry your great aunt is dead', people tend to use euphemisms in the form of verb phrases that are more sensitive and often barely relevant to the notion of death, such as 'passed on' or 'gone to a better place'. These are further supplemented by phatic platitudes such as 'sorry for your loss' that may not serve a genuine emotive function. People feel the need in emotionally charged situations to use language that is the least likely to cause offence or draw attention to the emotion. While this is socially acceptable and the norm in funerals, it can be seen as disingenuous, particularly to younger generations for whom emotional discussion – and, relevant to the first example above, 'calling out' discrimination – is considered more normal.

Arguably the focus on sensitivities and euphemistic language can obscure important issues that may be best brought out in the open. Consider aged-care facilities (Stimulus C) – the very name by which we know them skirts around their role in providing care to old people who are no longer able to care for themselves, essentially until they die. Rather than be blunt about their function, institutions set a precedent for a lack of clear information with the noun phrases that describe their role: 'residential institutions' or 'care facilities'. Some of the proper nouns given to these institutions include 'Waterford Valley Lakes', 'Glenhuntly Terrace' and 'Eliza Park', and their aim is to focus on an aspect of the facility such as its location, rather than its function, to shift the focus away from uncomfortable notions such as illness and dying. Unfortunately, this might facilitate both governments and organisations to obfuscate their responsibilities as these are kept out of sight by the bland language used to describe them. The Royal Commission into Aged Care Quality and Safety found that in aged care, 'people do not consistently receive the health care they need'. The active voice and explicit language draws attention to the lack of basic functionality in the system, which led to a public outcry that had been kept at bay by the systemic use of euphemism and obfuscation. While the government of the day and the organisations that offer poor care might feel the need to use euphemistic language, it is not always in the public interest.

Informally, on the other hand, euphemistic language can be used innovatively, and to build solidarity between interlocutors. Family members, for example, might enjoy sharing euphemisms about taboo topics, such as defecating, simply for the purposes of entertainment and fun: siblings might try to outwit one another by listing as many terms as they can, such as the metaphors 'laying some cable' or 'having a load to deliver'. Generally, even in informal situations, bodily functions will be discussed euphemistically. For example, women have a highly euphemistic 'moon time' or 'visit from Aunt Flo', or the more colourful but still oblique 'shark week' or 'crimson tide'. Even when there is a high level of intimacy between interlocutors, euphemistic language will still be deemed appropriate when talking about periods and poo. Conversely, the reputable toilet paper brand 'Who Gives a Crap' have used an informal dysphemism in their name to draw attention to the need for clean water and sanitation in developing countries. The name has a conative function to inspire purchasing the product to support their charity efforts. In this case, a euphemism is unnecessary and would detract from their sales purpose.

For a range of purposes, euphemisms are a common element of communication, though the necessity is arguable. While some formal contexts can certainly benefit from the use of euphemistic language, in some instances this is irrelevant or damaging. Informally, euphemism can be innovative and fun. Both formally and informally, there is a place for euphemism in successful communication in contemporary Australian society.

Question 7

'To achieve social cohesion, it is more important to be polite and considerate than it is to speak freely.'

To what extent is this true in contemporary Australian society? Refer to at least **two** subsystems of language in your response.

Possible approaches

This topic requires a discussion of the extent to which the language we use must be couched in terms of the rules of politeness and consideration in Australian society. Fundamentally, this is a discussion that will revolve around face needs and the understanding that to always speak freely will often threaten the face needs of those listening. Relevant elements of the course include Unit 3 Outcomes 1 and 2 in relation to the contextual influences on language, but also relevant are the outcomes in Unit 4, as often we deliberately choose to use language that will reflect a particular identity.

Responses could explore any of the following approaches.

- Consider the importance of politeness in relation to meeting the face needs of others, particularly when discussing sensitive or taboo topics. Stimulus A is particularly relevant as topics that were once part of everyday discourse have become increasingly sensitive.
- Consider the repercussions of violating sociocultural rules in relation to what can and cannot be discussed in public, in particular when understanding of social rules differs across individuals and groups. Stimulus D is relevant here as language has meaning 'filtered through our unique worldviews'.
- Consider the importance of acknowledging the rights and needs of others, particularly in relation to language of inclusion and non-discriminatory language. Stimulus C is particularly relevant here as public language requires an acknowledgement of the needs of individuals in 'diverse work environments'; public contexts most often require politeness and consideration.
- Consider how language rules can be flexible; being polite and considerate have a time and place, as does being able to freely express ideas without fear of repercussions. Stimulus B is particularly relevant here as what is considered polite and considerate can be quite different online when compared to face-to-face interactions. Online, people are also more likely to express their true opinions as they do not have the same fear of repercussions as they would in face-to-face interactions.
- Consider how there is a level of politeness and consideration that can be ignored online where interlocutors can be anonymous. As Stimulus B suggests, this can be dangerous and potentially offensive, damaging social cohesion.
- Consider the tendency for many online communities to be considered 'toxic', in that they deliberately provoke and harass others under the banner of 'free speech' while violating politeness rules and social norms. It is clear in these contexts, freedom of speech triumphs.
- Consider the idea that politeness and considerateness can be impossible to maintain all the time; often meeting the needs of one speaker can violate the needs of another. While it is important to be polite and considerate, you cannot achieve this with all people all of the time.

Sample response

In any civilised society, social cohesion is typically achieved through respectful discourse; being polite and considerate are two methods of creating and maintaining this respect. While it is often tempting to flout social rules and norms to express ourselves as we wish, this does not always help us in the longer term. It is therefore more important to be polite and considerate to others with the language that we use than it is to always express what we feel. That being said, there are times where the rules of politeness and consideration do not need to be adhered to for social cohesion to be achieved; adhering to social niceties is not the only method of creating positive social relationships.

Non-discriminatory language, by its definition, is language that is designed to avoid offence or disadvantage to members of particular groups. In this sense, non-discriminatory language achieves social cohesion as it is both polite and considerate to use language that will not alienate others. This is particularly the case in the workplace, where in the context of 'our diverse work environments' (Stimulus C) it is important to use language that is inclusive of others. Social distance in the workplace tends to be maintained at a professional level; therefore the language used in these environments should also remain professional. The importance of this is highlighted in Stimulus C, with the Victorian Government publishing an 'Inclusive Language Guide' so that all government employees understand the need for language to be used that 'empower[s] individuals and strengthen[s] relationships'. For example, when working with gender-diverse and non-binary co-workers, it is important that the correct pronouns are used to refer to colleagues. Similarly, Aboriginal and Torres Strait Islander people may prefer the use of the compound nouns 'brotherboy' or 'sistergirl' if they are transgender. The Victorian Government's Inclusive Language Guide outlines these examples of inclusive language. It is notable that a government body publishes such a guide, highlighting that in public language it is important to be polite and considerate in order to promote a cohesive society.

While politeness and consideration are important in face-to-face communication, there is increasing evidence that freedom of speech is triumphant in online communication. Social media websites such as Reddit provide opportunities for users to express their thoughts freely, often anonymously, without regard for the face needs of others. Some of the sub-groups on these sites actively seek to offend and denigrate others, violating social cohesion with the neologistic justification that it is done for the 'lulz' (a slang corruption of the acronym for 'laugh out loud'), where amusement is derived at the expense of others. In these communities, it is clearly not important for politeness and consideration to prevail, and instead it is the violation of social cohesion that is rewarded. There is an irony that to socially cohere in these online groups, one must violate the social norms of society rather than adhere to them.

The need to be polite and considerate dominates the public domain, but this is not necessarily the case in private settings. While a speaker must be careful as to what they say in public, in private there is a relaxation of social norms, reducing the need to be polite and considerate all the time. For example, I have many vegan friends who are passionate about veganism and animal conservation, and they are offended by idioms such as 'beating a dead horse' and 'letting the cat out of the bag' as they believe these phrases normalise violence towards animals. In conversations with them, it is important that I maintain social cohesion by avoiding such idioms, using euphemistic alternatives as suggested in Stimulus A, but when I am at home with my family, none of whom are vegan, I do not need to modify my language in the same way. Thus, while it is important to maintain politeness in some settings, there are just as many times where it is acceptable to speak freely.

It is clear that in many contexts, social cohesion is maintained through polite and respectful language. This is particularly so in public and professional contexts, where the importance of polite and considerate language is clear. Language 'can insult or encourage, smooth over misunderstandings or create rifts', but it is also very much the case that the intent of a speaker and the meaning behind what is said is 'filtered through our unique worldviews' (Stimulus D). Being able to freely express oneself can certainly triumph over needing to couch what is meant in polite and careful terms – for example, in contexts where violating social norms is encouraged. Similarly, intimacy often allows the stripping away of the norms required to achieve social cohesion, where it is acceptable to speak freely without fear of offence. In contemporary Australian society, then, it cannot be said that social cohesion can only be achieved through polite and considerate discourse; depending on the context, speaking freely can be just as successful.

Question 8

'Language change caused by technology has made it difficult to communicate effectively with each other.'

To what extent do you agree? Refer to at least **two** subsystems of language in your response.

Possible approaches

This topic requires an exploration of the role of technology in contributing to effective communication in society. Fundamentally, this is a discussion that will revolve around the prescriptive attitudes that exist about technology-driven language change. Relevant elements of the course include Unit 3 Outcomes 1 and 2 in relation to the contextual influences on language, such as the medium of its delivery, as well as how language is used to achieve various purposes. Also relevant are the outcomes in Unit 4, in particular when considering how language can help create an 'us versus them' mentality, forging solidarity while reinforcing social distance.

Responses could explore any of the following approaches.

- Consider the impact of technological innovations such as AI and moderation tools on lexemes and phrases as seen in Stimulus A, where social media users have to constantly invent code words to avoid potentially disagreeable content being filtered out by algorithms.
- Consider the view that technology-driven language change is a degradation of the English language, or – as in Stimulus B – that prescriptivists who dislike technology-based language change are irritating.

- Consider the idea that the driving force of language today is the 'agreement of the masses' (Stimulus C). There is no greater place for the 'masses' to meet than via the internet. Stimulus C suggests that the changing and shaping of language is controlled by the people.
- Consider the changing nature of punctuation due to the use of technology, as seen in Stimulus D. For example, the full stop can be used as a passive-aggressive method of showing dissatisfaction and hostility, which allows for subtle yet complex messages to be conveyed easily.

Sample response

The English language has always evolved, as without evolution a language quickly becomes obsolete. The rapid development in technology in the twenty-first century has caused the English language to evolve with unprecedented speed, far outpacing the rate of language change prior to this century. Communication more and more frequently occurs through online mediums rather than face-to-face interactions, and this serves to 'shrink' the world in relation to the introduction of new language forms. In this sense, much of this language change can seem unintelligible to those who have not immersed themselves in the online world, as the globalisation of communication leaves lexicographers rushing to codify new terms and expressions. Many prescriptivists lament these changes as a degradation of the English language, as once-fixed grammatical rules are seemingly ignored. However, language change attributed to technology can just as easily be viewed as enriching the English language, with the benefits of increasingly efficient communication far outweighing the potential for occasional misunderstanding.

The sheer speed with which new lexical forms are entering the English language can mostly be attributed to innovations in technology, particularly algorithms that enable content monitoring on social media platforms. Algospeak (Stimulus A) involves new lexical items or emojis being used as code words to bypass censorship of topics and issues that can occur on various social media platforms. For example, 'leg booty' is a stand-in for 'LGBTQ'. As new forms of language appear, it requires a dedication from the communicator to keep abreast of these changes to language forms, particularly when they involve complex codes or require a level of semantic decoding that can be confusing for those who are not familiar with the online communities that embrace this language form. This reduces the effectiveness with which one can communicate online as well. Without a firm knowledge of Standard English, it can be difficult to succeed in the modern world, and the more people are bombarded with non-standard language forms, the less likely they are able to detect, construct and manipulate standard language forms themselves. This reduces their likelihood of being able to communicate effectively with others outside of their online communities.

The world is shrinking. The advancement of technology and online communication makes it easier to communicate with others on a global scale, but this does not come without cost. Communicating in a globalised world requires effective language use, and this in turn places a duty of care on a speaker or writer to carefully construct their language so as not to exclude others. Rather than creating an efficient method of communication, then, technology promotes such swift changes to language that misspeaking and misinterpretation are inevitable. While the neologistic contranym 'literally' may not necessarily cause confusion, because it is generally understood from the context as to whether the literal or figurative meaning is meant, other culturally based contranyms can hinder clear communication. Consider the idiomatic phrase 'lucked out', which traditionally in Australia and the United Kingdom means to be 'out of luck', while in North America it means 'to be lucky'. These antonymic meanings can cause confusion and offence when communicating online. For example, if providing congratulations to an American couple at their wedding, it would be entirely appropriate to state that one had 'lucked out' when they met their now-spouse, but in Australia and the UK, this would be very poorly received. It is therefore safer to not use colloquial phrases such as these, but that places the onus on all communicators to be well versed in the myriad meanings of every word they utter across multiple continents when communicating cross-culturally – not something that is realistically achievable. While technology provides an efficient method of communication, it cannot be said that it always provides an effective one.

While the speed at which new language forms are entering the language can be overwhelming, the language changes that have been attributed to technology are not always ineffective. Consider the speed with which one can communicate with others through introduced language forms such as emojis and emoticons, and the repurposing of punctuation. The power of punctuation can be seen in Stimulus D, where the final panel humorously shows the female responding with punctuative hostility to the male's explanations in the previous panels. This hostility is clear due to the changed nature of punctuation in online communication; full stops are frequently seen as abrupt, often hostile, closings to conversational turns. Similarly, the ease with which people informally communicate using only emojis was most notably demonstrated by former foreign minister Julie Bishop, who in 2015 answered interview questions on Channel 9's *Today* show with facial expressions mimicking emojis. More recently, in 2017, Deakin University researcher Dr Adam Brown promoted emojis for their success in allowing for paralinguistic and prosodic features of speech, such as gesture and intonation, to be more easily integrated into written texts. Technological language change has therefore provided a powerful tool to its users in allowing some of the limitations of written language to be overcome, promoting more effective communication.

As Rentoul writes in Stimulus B, 'language changes', and despite some people thinking that 'the new usage is "wrong"', the willing adoption of these changes to language by so many seems to suggest that this is not the case. When considering the effectiveness of communication, technology has provided a medium by which people can communicate quickly and efficiently with others on a global scale. With this, however, comes the inevitable confusion that arises when cultural differences in language use collide. While technology has resulted in lightning-fast changes to language, as Buxton writes in Stimulus C, 'language works by agreement of the masses', and as more and more users become proficient in the use of new language forms, perhaps the effectiveness of communication will increase. At this stage, however, it cannot be said that technology has had a wholly positive impact on the effectiveness of communication, particularly in relation to cross-cultural communication.

Question 9

'Jargon is unnecessarily complicated language used to impress, rather than to inform, your audience.'

To what extent do you agree? Refer to at least **two** subsystems of language in your response.

Possible approaches

As this is a 'To what extent do you agree?' topic, it requires some evaluation of the pros and cons of the use of jargon. Students should recognise that the appropriate use of jargon depends on context. Students need to understand that although the term 'jargon' sometimes has negative connotations in our society, there are positives to its use in some aspects of our daily life. The topic requires knowledge of both Units 3 and 4 as jargon often serves a function in more formal contexts, but it is also closely linked with expression and reflection of identity.

Responses could explore any of the following approaches.

- All professions and jobs require the use of jargon to some extent.
- Jargon allows for effective communication among experts in a specific field, ensuring accuracy, precision, and avoiding unproductive discussions with those who do not have domain knowledge or interest.
- The shared identity it can create gives a sense of solidarity with users of a specific field of jargon, including interests such as sport or other pastimes.
- Jargon can reflect a professional identity for the user; this can be seen as a positive or negative.
- Jargon can exclude those who do not understand it, therefore its use could be a face-threatening act.
- Jargon can be used deliberately to confuse, obfuscate or hide the truth as seen in advertising, the military and politics.
- Some users of jargon may deliberately use it to project a particular identity which may be intended to exclude or put down others.

Sample response

Language undoubtedly has a number of functions in our society and can be employed in myriad ways. It is true that jargon can be unnecessarily complicated, used to exclude others and can make a speaker sound arrogant or indirect. However, in many contexts, jargon is a useful shortcut that promotes effective communication, creates a sense of belonging and can produce a trustworthy identity for the user. In addition, there is now more widespread understanding and use of some jargon, leading to its standardisation and giving power to users to express ideas in more nuanced ways, and even to promote social cohesion.

In some contexts, jargon can facilitate successful communication as it is precise and efficient. As a result, those using it in a particular speech community can experience a sense of belonging. The study of many VCE subjects, including English Language, relies on jargon to inform students about concepts relating to the subject in a lexically condensed way. An example of this would be the noun 'predicate'; if one were to explain this term to someone who had little to no knowledge of linguistics, it would require considerable detail in the explanation. However, in the English Language classroom, a member of the class can use this one lexical item in a piece of discourse and quickly move to the next point. Jargon is not only used in education and professions such as medicine or law, but it is used in sport for a range of purposes. It is a way to quickly relay the action to the audience, to reflect the speaker's expertise, and to allow interlocutors to freely converse about their shared interest. It can also lead to creating a sense of in-group belonging. Over the Australian summer, cricket is broadcast via a range of media sources and jargon is a common factor in the discourse. On ABC Radio, a commentator relayed the action to their listening audience through a number of declaratives that contained jargon: 'leg-spinner Khan has taken a third wicket, taps it to the third man, a short ball off the stump.' To anyone not familiar with cricket, utterances such as the nouns 'stump' and 'leg-spinner' and the noun phrase 'the third man' do not mean much but, to cricket enthusiasts, the commentator keeps them informed of the action as it is happening through the use of cricket-specific language; they trust that the commentator knows what they are talking about as they have employed the 'right' language in this context. This complex, jargon-driven language plays a key role in creating effective, informative communication and would not be seen by the audience as impressive, but in fact appropriate and necessary.

In addition to the role that jargon can play in education, workplaces, and sport, it has also promoted a sense of cohesion because when these 'special words or expressions that are used by a particular profession' (Stimulus A) occur in mainstream speech communities, they become Standard. Important issues in society today include the environment and the economy; therefore, terms that would have typically been used by professionals in these fields, including politicians, start to be used more widely. Most Australians know the meaning of jargonistic noun phrases such as 'biodegradable waste' and 'zero emissions' as our environment is constantly in the media, particularly in times of bushfire crisis. In addition, economical terms 'supply and demand' and 'budgetary policy' make sense to the general population and the semantic broadening of 'equilibrium' and 'awards' can be seen with additional economical definitions added to the dictionary. This standardisation and sometimes codification reflect current issues and interests in contemporary society. Having the ability to discuss them in a broader context enables speakers to be informed, and to inform others.

However, it is understandable that jargon is often criticised as it can be confusing and exclusionary. Some speakers employ jargon to present a particular identity of someone who might be more educated or might have more knowledge in a particular field. Stimulus C demonstrates an instance when jargon is used to project a particular identity while at the same time excluding the intended recipient of the information. The nouns 'aortic root' and 'aortic cusps', and the adjectives 'stenotic' and 'tricuspid' may have little to no meaning to a patient. Yet these words are content words and the function of content words is to provide meaning. As well as impeding its referential function, jargon can also obfuscate. This is often most apparent when our politicians are speaking. Governments install 'safety cameras' that provide revenue through fines, a fact that is obfuscated by the adjective choice. New taxes are referred to as 'deficit levies' or 'co-payments' to avoid the lexeme 'tax'. Stuart Robert, the former Minister for Government Services, tweeted a long and mostly indecipherable thread towards the end of 2019. A section of it read: 'architecture allows us to build an ontology of capabilities'. Presumably Robert aimed to confuse his audience with impressive-sounding terms that prevented them from understanding that the government had little to show for their digitised services, thus taking away the public's power to react or question him on this matter. Jargon that is used to make the user appear more informed or more educated rather than to inform is a face-threatening act, as the audience feels excluded and possibly unintelligent or ill-informed.

Jargon can play an important role in many contexts, such as when it facilitates communication or allows the general public to discuss matters of societal importance, but it can also hinder or inhibit effective communication. If jargon is being used to project a particular identity at the expense of others or to muddy the waters, then it is not fulfilling its intended function.

Question 10

'While seemingly open to language change and variation, we still judge others based on how they use language.'

Is this true in the context of contemporary Australian society? Refer to at least **two** subsystems of language in your response.

Possible approaches

As this is an 'Is this true?' topic, it requires some comment on both sides of the topic. There has been greater acceptance of non-discriminatory language to manage the face needs of others. There has also been a greater acceptance of cultural varieties, with ethnolects and Aboriginal Australian Englishes being seen and heard more and more in the media. Younger people use more and more textspeak, which is acceptable and almost expected in their social groups. However, there are still members of society who will judge others based on their language use or will not accept change due to prescriptivist or old-fashioned views. Over time attitudes towards 'Aussie' language have changed, with more Australians speaking with a General accent and avoiding some of the more stereotypical Australian colloquialisms. A sound understanding of both Units 3 and 4 is needed for this question to be able to discuss language in Australia in terms of variation according to context, purpose and identity.

Responses could explore any of the following:

- the shift to using more non-discriminatory language in relation to marginalised communities in Australia, and how, conversely, there are members of our society who will speak out against this type of language
- changes due to technology and the prevalent use of internet speak, which is viewed favourably by the users but not by those who might hold more prescriptivist views when it comes to language
- the rise of migrant ethnolects and Aboriginal Australian Englishes in private and public contexts, which indicates more acceptance by those outside of these groups, although there will still be some who view these as inferior varieties of English

- individuals breaking away from the Australian stereotype due to less favourable judgements towards those who speak with Broad or Cultivated accents
- differing opinions on the language features of particular groups, including uptalk or business jargon
- the act of judging is not always negative, as we can judge someone as belonging to our in-group through their language.

Sample response

While modern Australia appears to be a more tolerant and inclusive society, with our language reflecting this, it is not hard to find examples of people judging others for the way they speak or write English. In the Australian context we have seen changes that reflect our ideas of what is considered non-discriminatory language, particularly in relation to marginalised communities, but there are always some who see this shift in language as taking things too far. As well as this, Australia's cultural make-up has changed over time with the emergence of other variants of Australian English such as migrant ethnolects and improved awareness of Aboriginal Australian Englishes. Though most Australians see these ethnocultural additions in a positive light, there are others who still view them as 'broken English' (Stimulus A). Even the Australian accent has not avoided criticism, with many of us favouring the General Australian accent due to less favourable views towards the Broad and Cultivated variants. Further to this, stereotypical 'Aussie' colloquial language is also no longer as popular with younger Australians. Therefore, while we are generally open to change and variation when it comes to language, it cannot be said that we maintain this attitude all of the time.

In Australia, we have seen changes in public language that reflect changing social attitudes, including using more inclusive and non-discriminatory language in a range of contexts. Reviewed in September 2020, the LGBTIQ+ Inclusive Language Guide from the Victorian Government explains to members of the public sector how to 'use language respectfully and inclusively' when working with and referring to members of our community. There is also reference to not assuming a person's gender identification (Stimulus D) as some people use a gender-neutral pronoun such as 'they'. When governments make these public changes, it contributes to moving the prestige from covert to overt and thus normalising the use of inclusive language. Many Australian schools now have policies that use 'they' when referring to the students instead of the previous policy that used 'him/her'; these changes are supported by school communities. That said, despite official documents such as the Australian Government Style Manual recommending against using gendered terms such as 'policeman' and 'actress', Nine News referred to Australian actors Nicole Kidman and Rose Byrne as 'actresses' in a report about celebrities moving to Australia in 2021. So while we have seen progress in using inclusive and gender-neutral language in Australia, there are people and organisations who might not have moved with the times or reject guidelines.

With more people relocating to Australia from all parts of the world and greater acceptance of the languages of our First Nations peoples, Australian English is changing due to these cultural influences, and society is generally accepting of these changes. In many contexts, Australians see and hear other languages being used, such as the popular 'Yiayia Next Door' Instagram page. The Greek noun 'yiayia' means 'grandmother', but that does not need explaining to the 75 000 followers of this Instagram account because it is a term familiar to many, with Australia home to one of the largest Greek communities in the world (*The Herald Sun*, 2017). In addition, in a May 2020 ABC interview featuring Essendon women's football star and Noongar woman Courtney Ugle, she talked about her 'tiddas' and 'mob' when referring to her Aboriginal sisters and people. Those in the audience who were not Indigenous did not judge Ugle for her use of non-standard English. They have had increased exposure to Aboriginal Australian Englishes via our televisions, radio and social media platforms and they understand the importance of First Nations people using their language in the public domain. Despite this growing acceptance of cultural factors in our language, there is still a notion that these varieties are 'broken English' (Stimulus A) and many migrants or children of migrant parents do not feel they fit in because of this. Sonia Nair, a Melbourne-based writer with a Malaysian background, commented in an article for SBS that she was told her English is good 'despite where [she'd] come from' and expressed her experience of the need to sound 'like an Australian' to fit in, reflecting the country's continuing racism and ignorance. A friend of mine who is of Aboriginal and Torres Strait Islander background will often joke about the way her family uses language in their family chats, referring to it as 'pidgin English' when they write things such as the verb phrase 'lak led', meaning 'is best'. As is so often the case, contemporary Australia's acceptance of linguistic differences is in fact a reflection of our acceptance of cultural differences and thus the opinions of both individuals and groups vary.

Overseas, Australia is affectionately known for its linguistic innovation and Broad accent; however, this language is not always regarded with the same affection within Australia. Old-school Australian exports such as Paul Hogan (*Crocodile Dundee*) and Steve Irwin uttered colloquial Australian idioms and phrases such as 'flat out like a lizard drinkin' and 'crikey' in typically Broad Australian accents. Their /ɑe/ diphthong in lexemes such as the 'i' in 'high' sounded more like /oɪ/ (as in 'toy'). Though this image sold well to the international market, urban Australia's perception of people who speak like this is not so favourable. They are viewed as being from less-educated, working-class backgrounds, with politicians such as Pauline Hanson and Barnaby Joyce employing such language features and receiving criticism. Moreover, these two do not hold to the same values of inclusiveness as those held by many Australians who cluster in the larger cities like Melbourne; thus, the language used marks Australians as insiders or outsiders, urban or rural, progressive or 'true blue'. As a result, many Australians diverge from sounding like the stereotype, following Giles' Communication Accommodation Theory that individuals' linguistic styles converge with those around them. The same can be said for the Cultivated accent at the other end of the spectrum. Our attitude to speakers of this variety of Australian English is that they are stuck-up and do not align with the modern egalitarian national identity that has been developed over years. A Cultivated speaker might be identified by their more British-sounding accent, such as former politician Malcolm Turnbull, who, in an ABC Radio National interview, pronounced the adjective 'vitally' with a strong /t/ phoneme and the noun 'pseudonym' with the palatal approximant /j/ following the initial /s/ phoneme. In 2018, a Monash University study claimed that the Cultivated accent has become 'less relevant' and carries 'less social capital'. Judgements towards both varieties are said to be why most Australians speak with the General accent and tend not to utter some of the stereotypical colloquialisms of the past. The General accent is uniquely Australian but 'without the undesirable connotations associated with either the Cultivated or Broad accents' (Macquarie).

In recent times, Australia's language has changed, with most of us employing the General Australian accent with variances according to our cultural heritage, values and geography. We are more aware of the power of language and therefore make more of an effort to manage face needs by using non-discriminatory terminology. Generally, Australians accept these changes and variants as they are a marker of identity. Despite this, there are still prejudices toward other varieties, including accents from each end of the continuum of Australian English.

Acknowledgements

Insight Publications thanks Prudence Meggitt for reviewing and substantial writing contributions, and Siegrid Fischer for reviewing this resource.

Insight Publications thanks the following writers for their contributions to this resource: Selina Dennis, Georgie Jones, David Martin, Louise Noonan, Olivia Shenken, Rebecca Swain.

Insight Publications is also grateful to the following individuals and organisations for permission to reproduce copyright material.

The ABC for

- 'QandA Teaching Special'
- 'Australia has been called a "graveyard of languages". These people are bucking the trend' by Masako Fukui
- 'Aboriginal English recognition in schools critical for improving student outcomes for Indigenous Australians' by Madison Snow
- 'triple j's Hottest 100 is moving to a new date and here's why' by triple j.

The Copyright Agency and

- *The Age* for 'We should dare to dream of a Docklands that isn't dreadful' by *The Age*'s View
- *The Sydney Morning Herald* for 'How Succession saved the English Language' by David Astle.

Additional images by Melisa Paredes and sourced from Shutterstock.

Note: Some sources and sample responses were originally written in previous years and so may refer to events set in the past.